MANDALAS
AS A TOOL FOR TRANSFORMATION:

HOW THEY CAN HELP YOU CHANGE YOUR LIFE FOR THE BETTER

SMORODIN.STUDIO

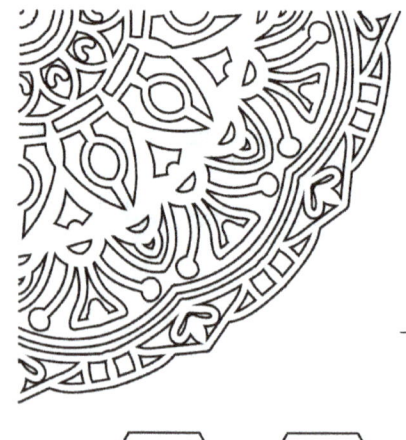
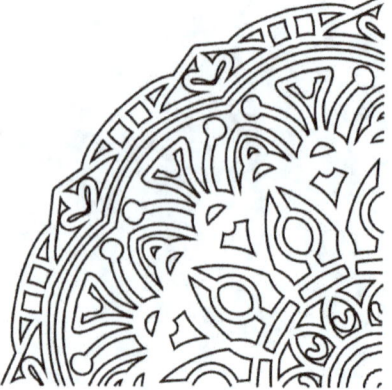

TEST COLOR PAGE

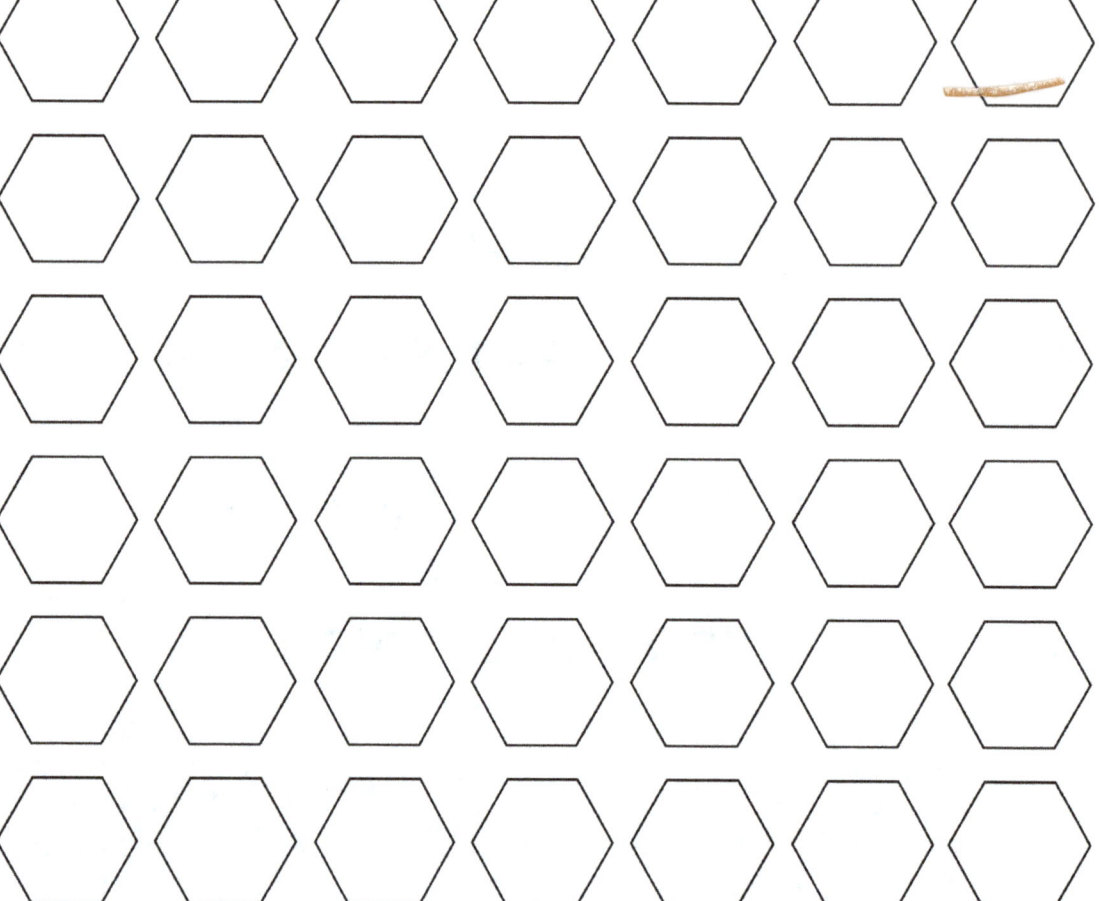

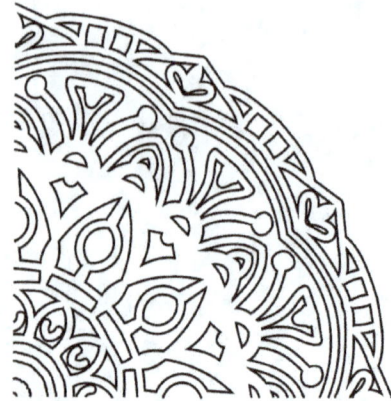

SMORODIN.STUDIO

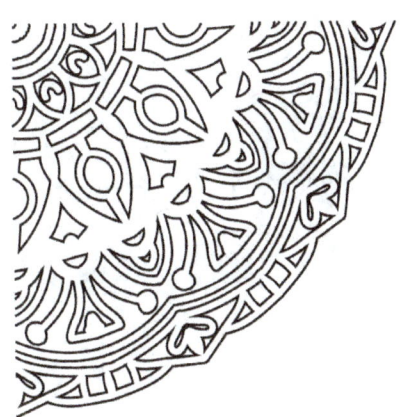
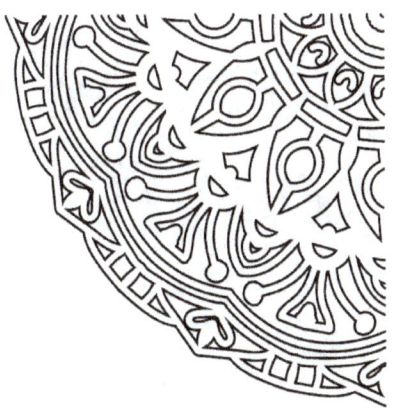

Mandalas have been used for centuries as a form
of self-expression, discovery, and healing.
When you create a mandala, you are tapping into your
subconscious and conscious selves to create a work of art that
reflects your mental, emotional, and spiritual well-being.

Creating a mandala can be very therapeutic and can
help to soothe chaotic psychological states.
If you are feeling stressed, anxious, or depressed,
try sitting down and creating a mandala.
You might be surprised at how much better you feel afterwards.

When creating mandalas, there are no rules.
You can draw symmetrical patterns or fill the circle
with shapes and colors in any way you like.
It is entirely up to you to decide how your mandala will look.

Creating mandalas:
* Relaxes the body and mind
* Cultivates happiness, inner peace, and general well-being
* Eases stress, anxiety, worry, overwhelm, fear, depression
* Activates creativity and improves focus
* Enhances self-esteem and self-acceptance
* Fosters a sense of connectedness with oneself and others
* Improves sleep

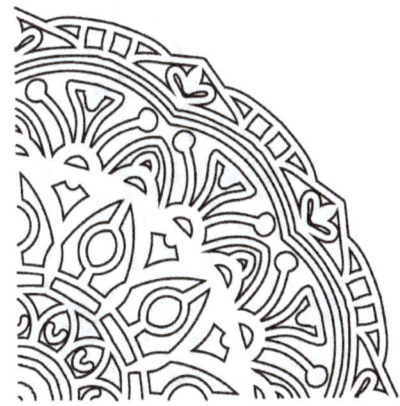
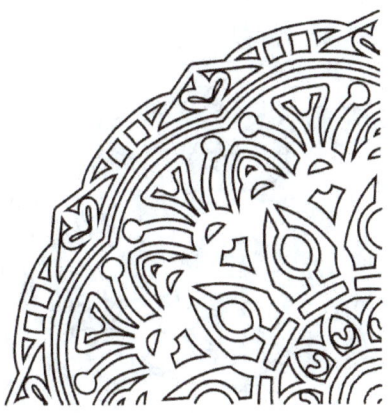

smorodin.studio

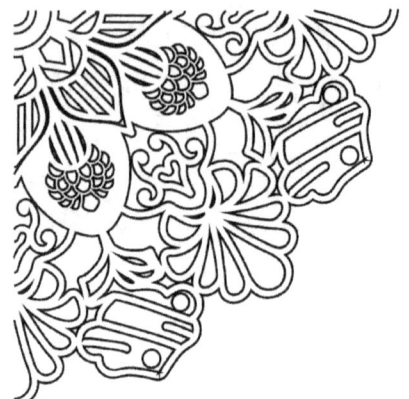
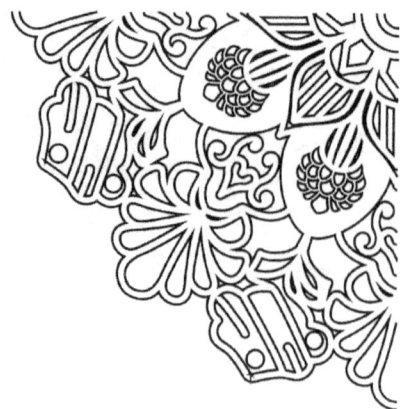

MANDALA #01

Coloring a mandala, is a great way to tune into our subconscious and see what emotional and mental state we are in.

These 3 steps will allow you to create a personal mandala:

1. Find a comfortable place to work. Sit in a quiet place where you won't be interrupted. Concentrate on the problem you want to solve the most in the moment.

2. Fill the shape with colors that reflect your current state of mind. Let your imagination run wild. There are no rules when creating a mandala.

3. Take some time to reflect on your mandala and what it means to you, and write down the result below.

_____

_____

_____

_____

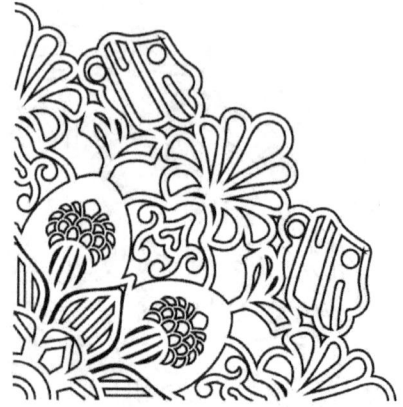

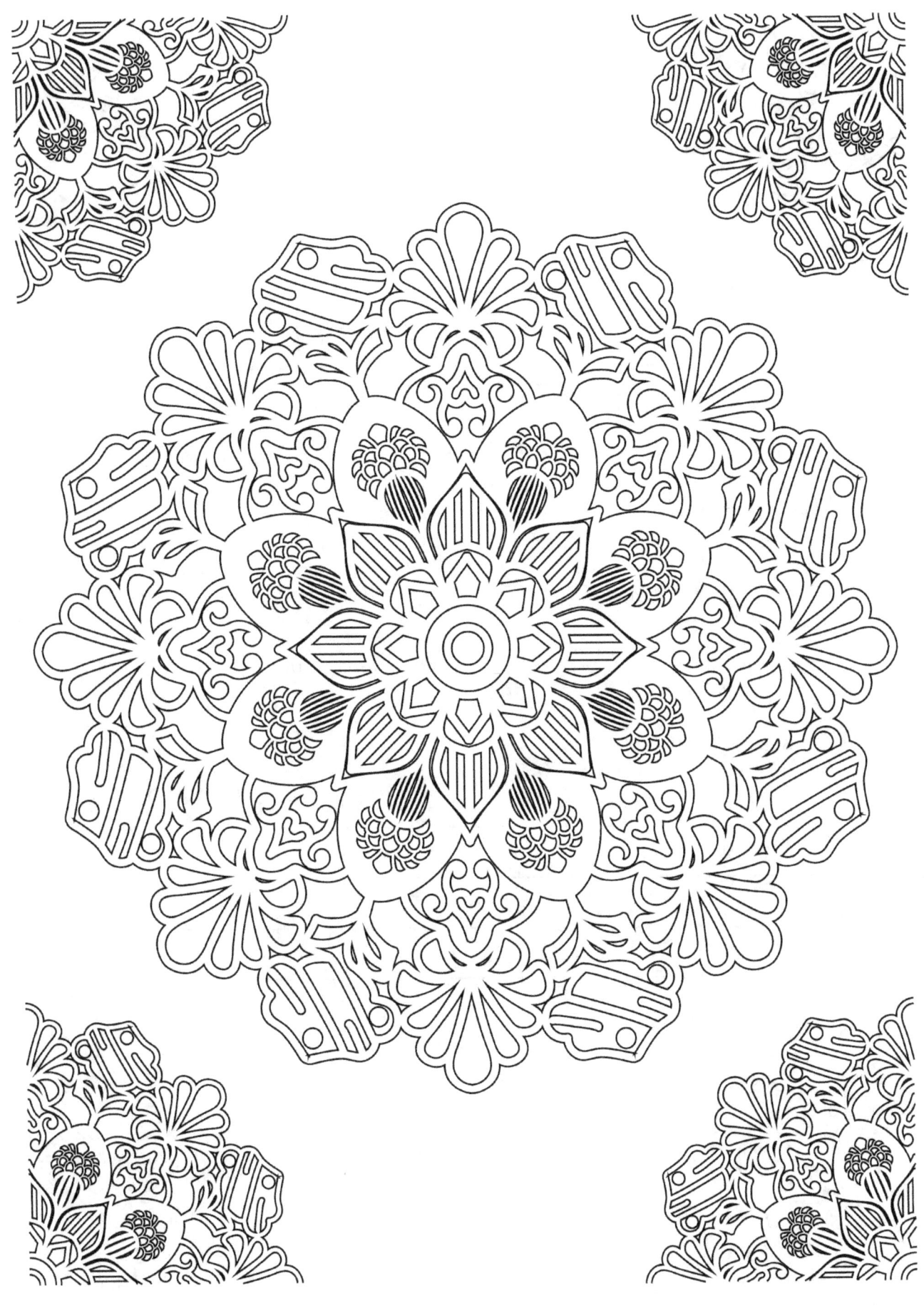

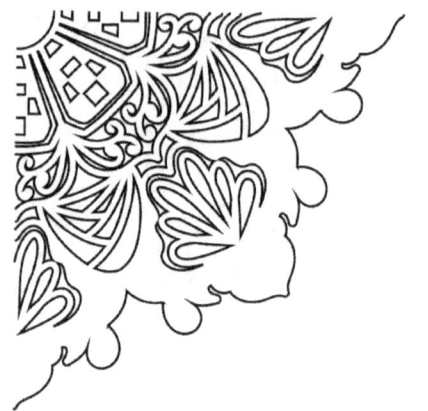
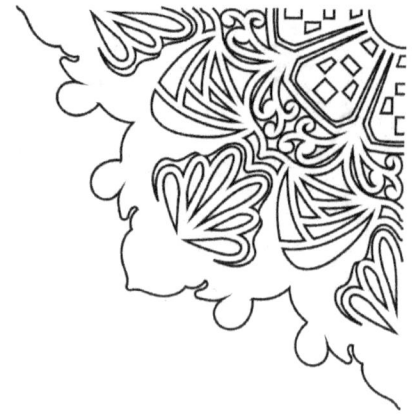

MANDALA #02

Coloring a mandala, is a great way to tune into our subconscious and see what emotional and mental state we are in.
These 3 steps will allow you to create a personal mandala:

1. Find a comfortable place to work. Sit in a quiet place where you won't be interrupted. Concentrate on the problem you want to solve the most in the moment.

2. Fill the shape with colors that reflect your current state of mind. Let your imagination run wild. There are no rules when creating a mandala.

3. Take some time to reflect on your mandala and what it means to you, and write down the result below.

_____
_____
_____
_____

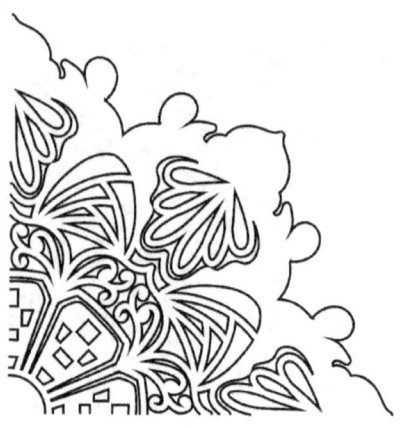
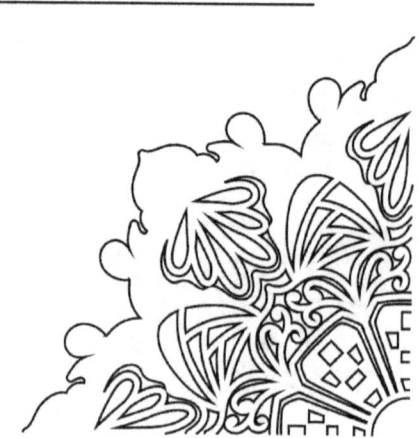

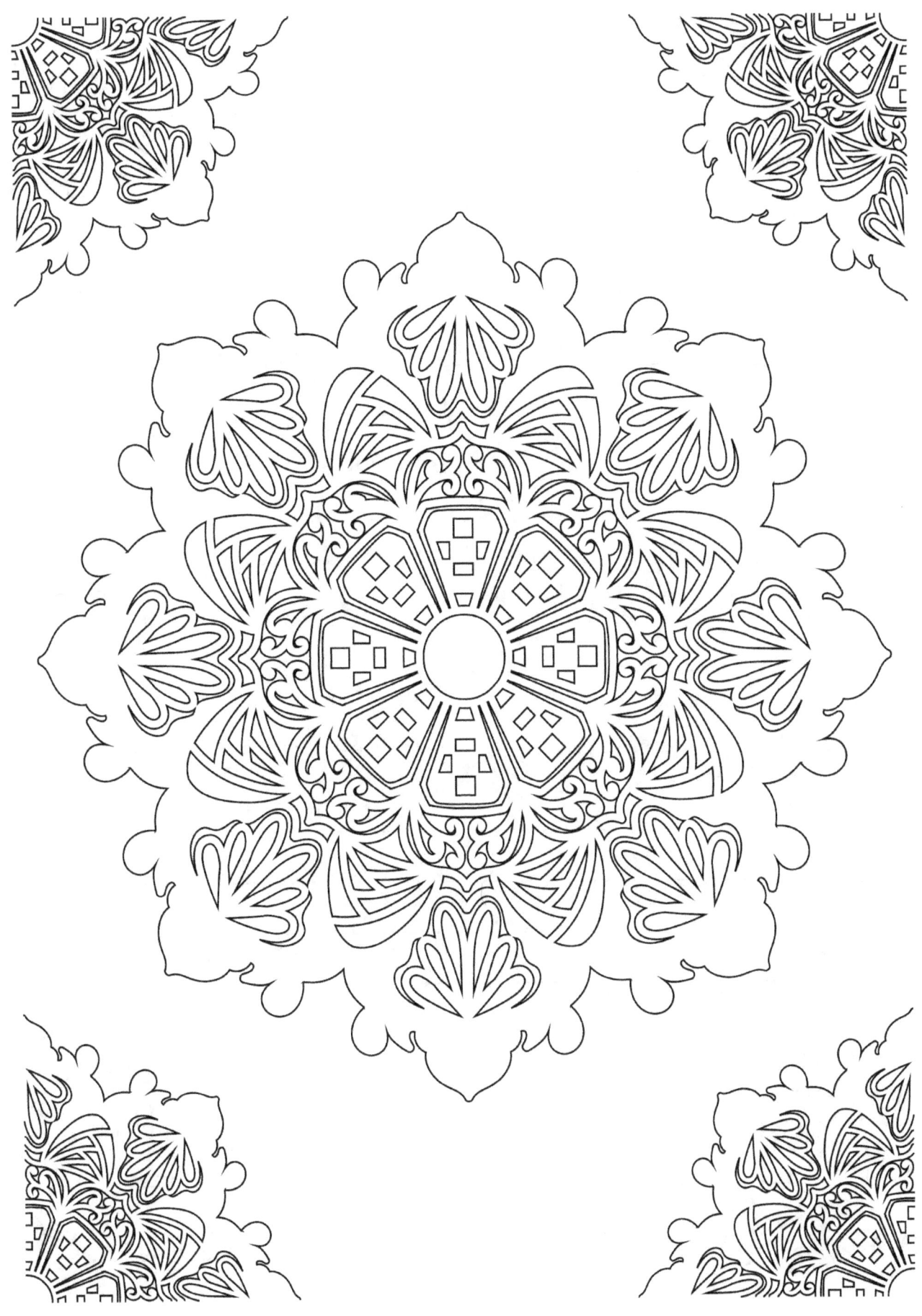

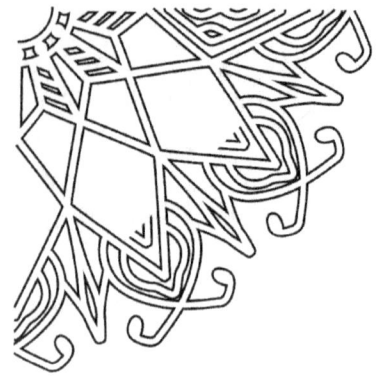
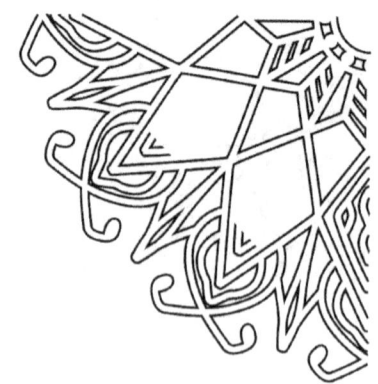

MANDALA #03

Coloring a mandala, is a great way to tune into our subconscious and see what emotional and mental state we are in.

These 3 steps will allow you to create a personal mandala:

1. Find a comfortable place to work. Sit in a quiet place where you won't be interrupted. Concentrate on the problem you want to solve the most in the moment.

2. Fill the shape with colors that reflect your current state of mind. Let your imagination run wild. There are no rules when creating a mandala.

3. Take some time to reflect on your mandala and what it means to you, and write down the result below.

_____
_____
_____
_____

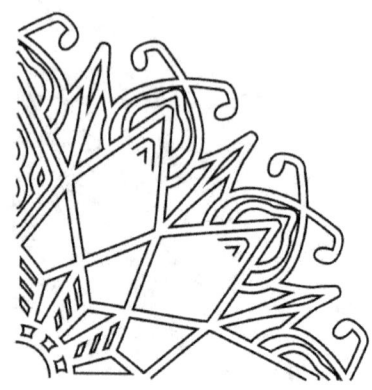
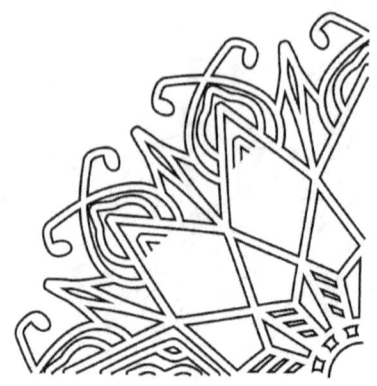

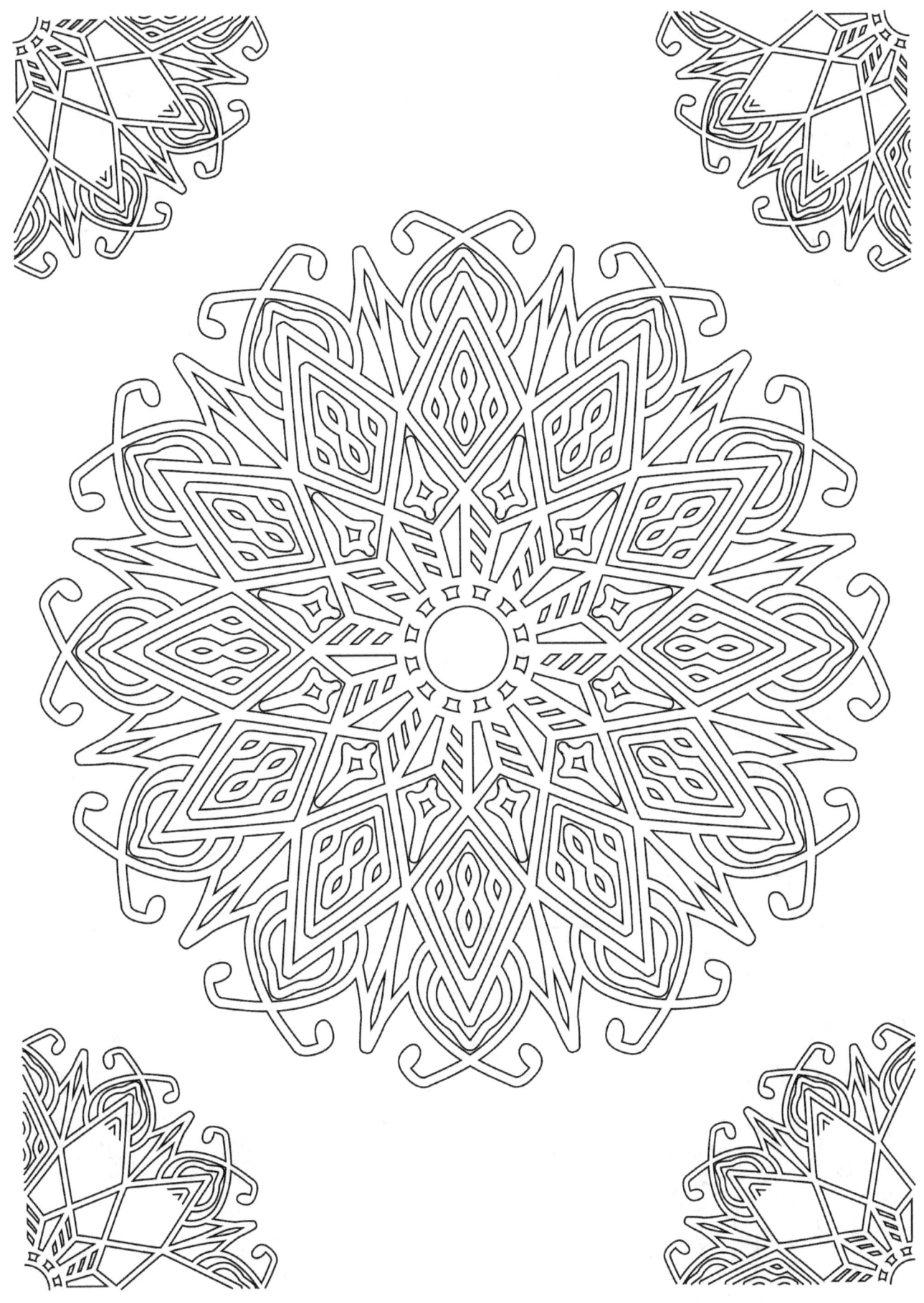

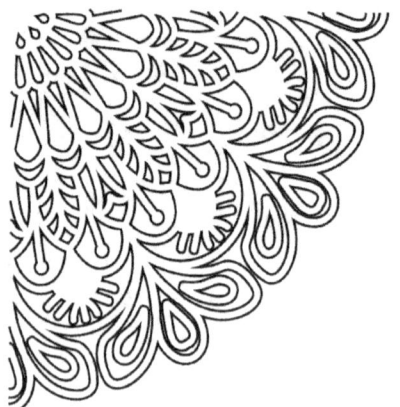
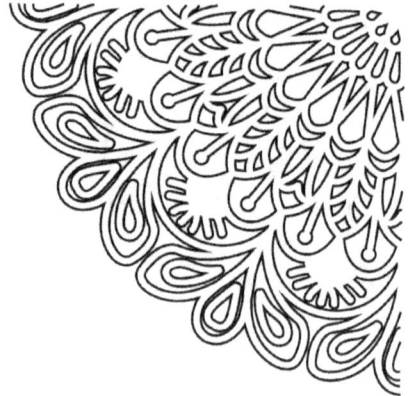

MANDALA #04

Coloring a mandala, is a great way to tune into our subconscious and see what emotional and mental state we are in.
These 3 steps will allow you to create a personal mandala:

1. Find a comfortable place to work. Sit in a quiet place where you won't be interrupted. Concentrate on the problem you want to solve the most in the moment.

2. Fill the shape with colors that reflect your current state of mind. Let your imagination run wild. There are no rules when creating a mandala.

3. Take some time to reflect on your mandala and what it means to you, and write down the result below.

_____
_____
_____
_____

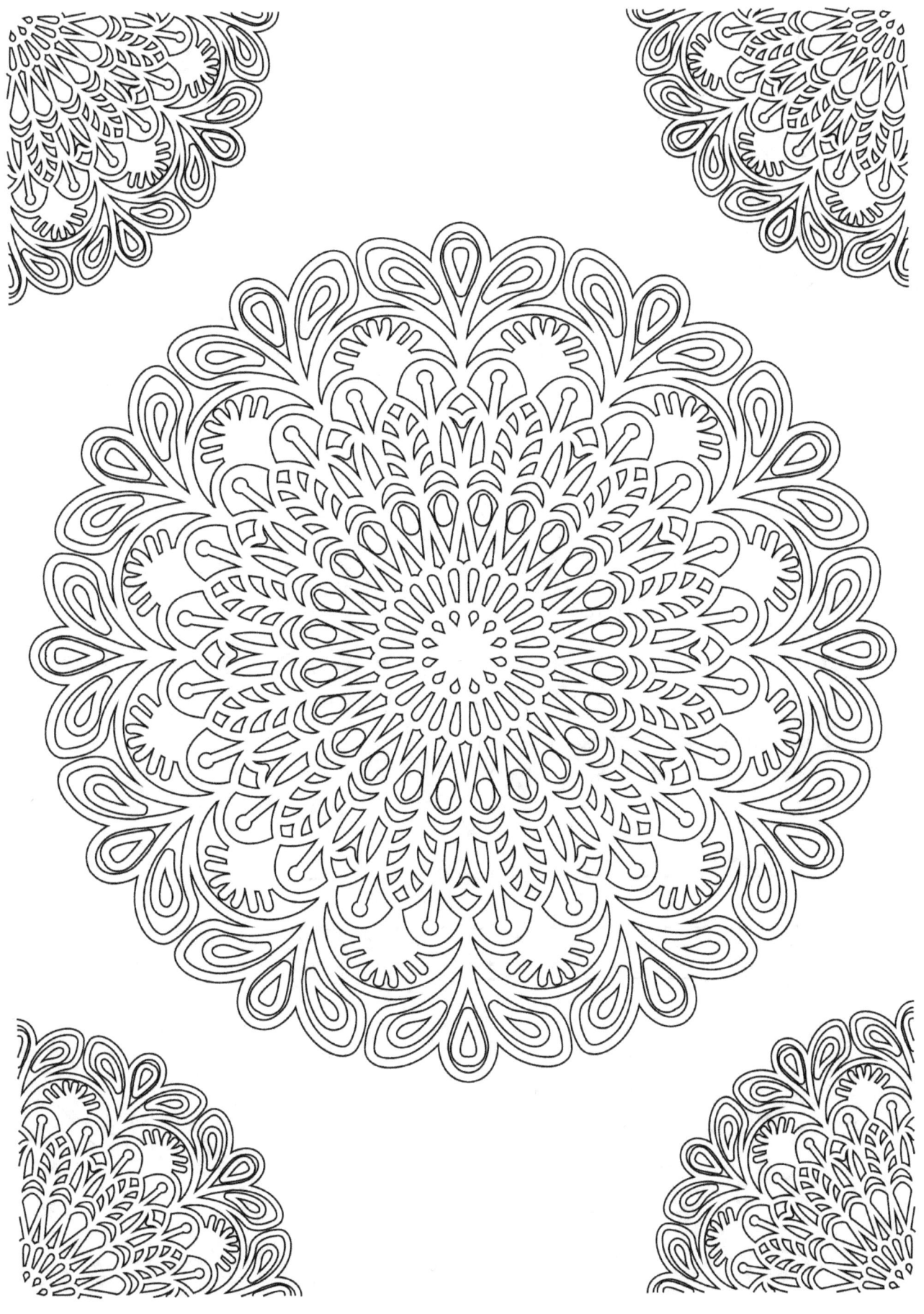

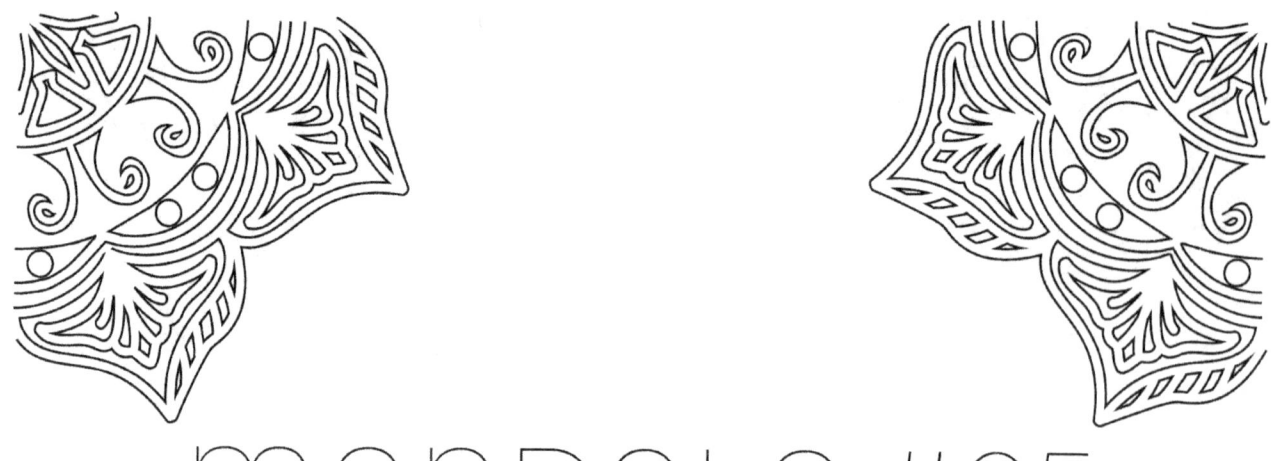

MANDALA #05

Coloring a mandala, is a great way to tune into our subconscious and see what emotional and mental state we are in.

These 3 steps will allow you to create a personal mandala:

1. Find a comfortable place to work. Sit in a quiet place where you won't be interrupted. Concentrate on the problem you want to solve the most in the moment.

2. Fill the shape with colors that reflect your current state of mind. Let your imagination run wild. There are no rules when creating a mandala.

3. Take some time to reflect on your mandala and what it means to you, and write down the result below.

_____
_____
_____
_____

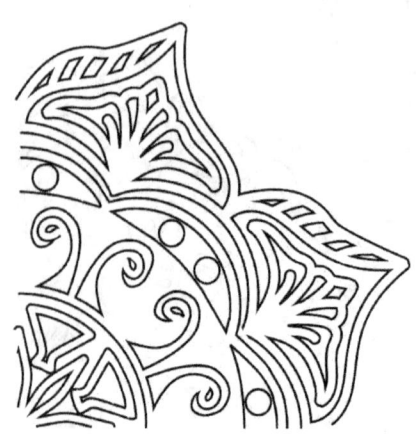

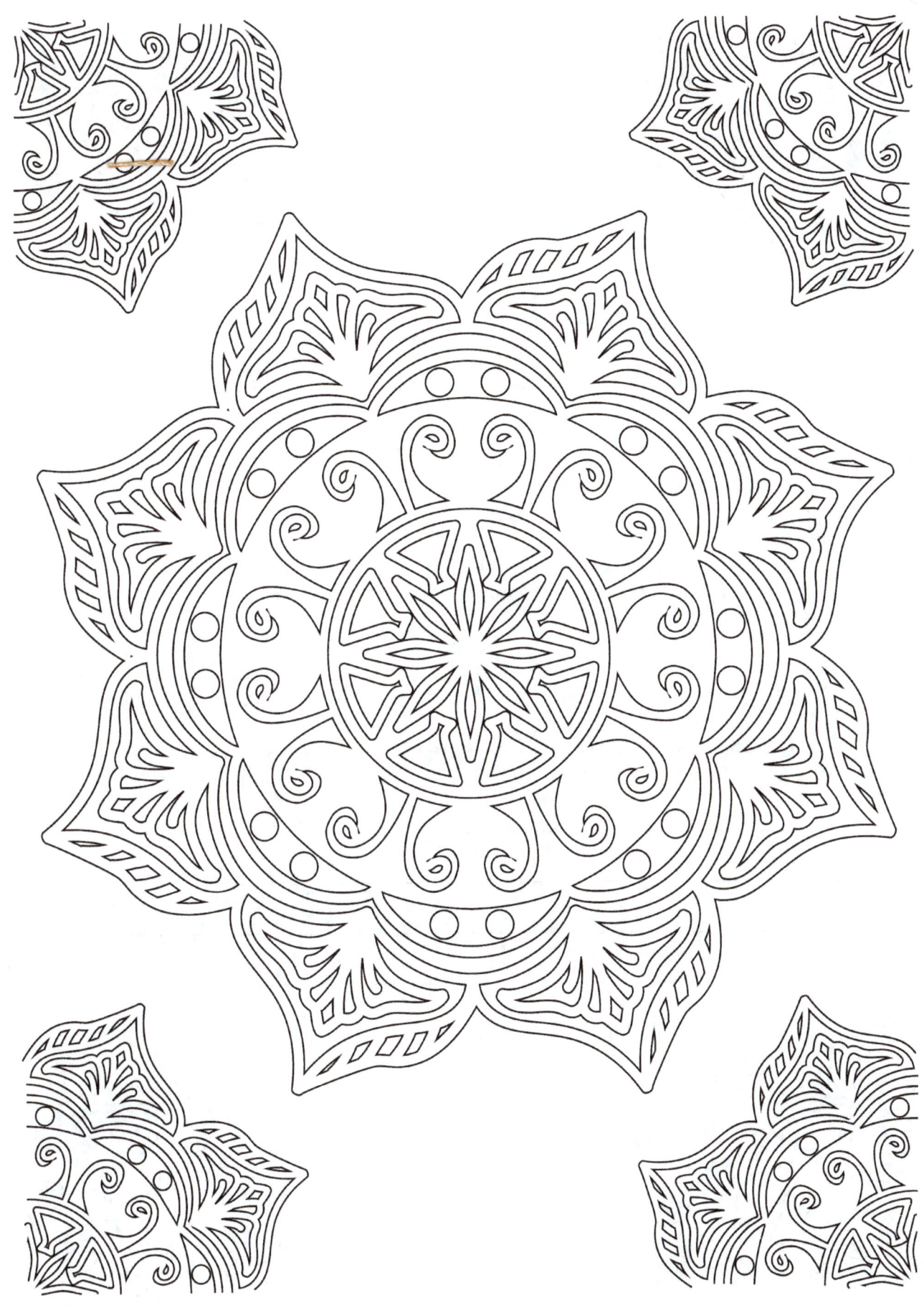

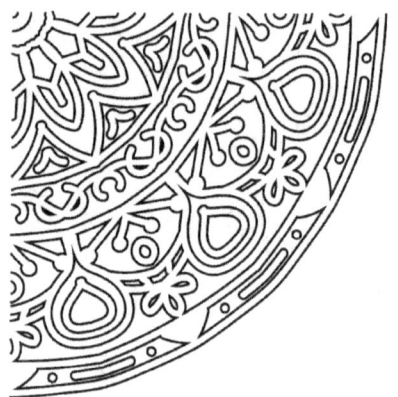
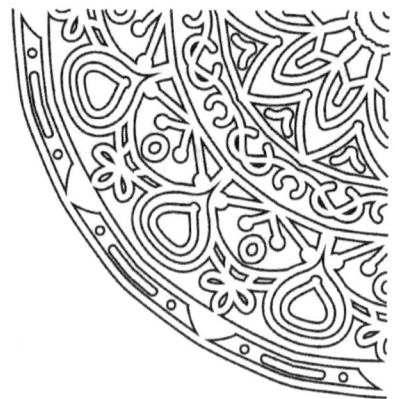

MANDALA #06

Coloring a mandala, is a great way to tune into our subconscious and see what emotional and mental state we are in.
These 3 steps will allow you to create a personal mandala:

1. Find a comfortable place to work. Sit in a quiet place where you won't be interrupted. Concentrate on the problem you want to solve the most in the moment.

2. Fill the shape with colors that reflect your current state of mind. Let your imagination run wild. There are no rules when creating a mandala.

3. Take some time to reflect on your mandala and what it means to you, and write down the result below.

_____
_____
_____
_____

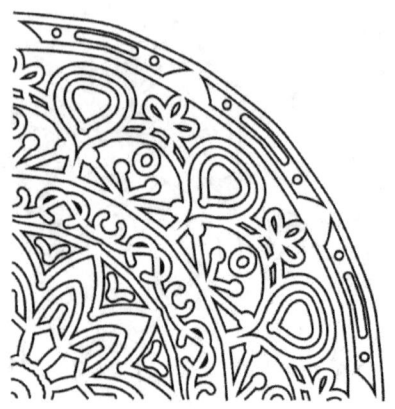
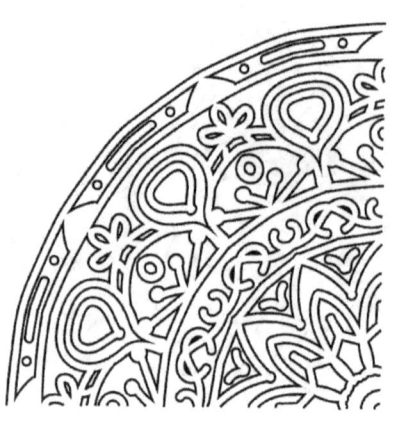

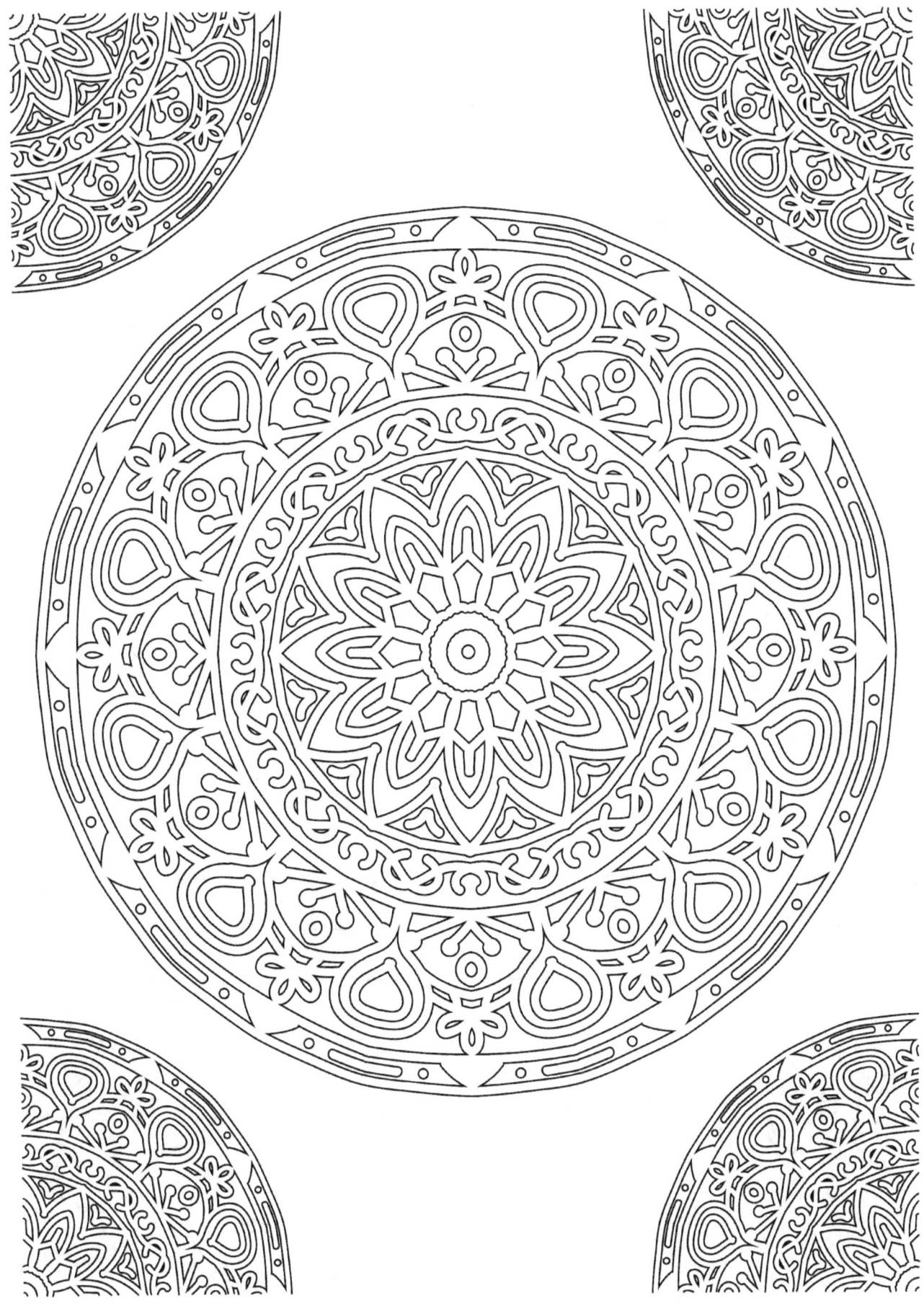

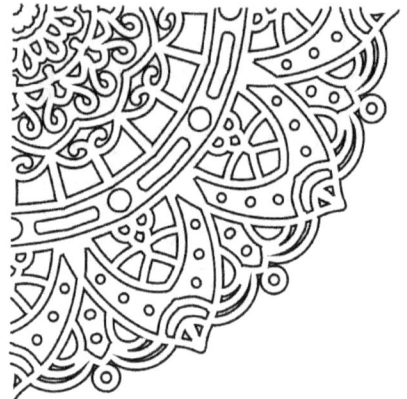
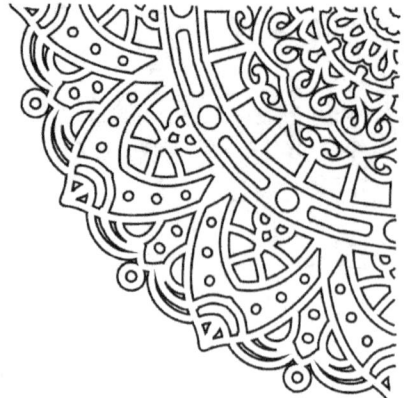

MANDALA #07

Coloring a mandala, is a great way to tune into our subconscious and see what emotional and mental state we are in.

These 3 steps will allow you to create a personal mandala:

1. Find a comfortable place to work. Sit in a quiet place where you won't be interrupted. Concentrate on the problem you want to solve the most in the moment.

2. Fill the shape with colors that reflect your current state of mind. Let your imagination run wild. There are no rules when creating a mandala.

3. Take some time to reflect on your mandala and what it means to you, and write down the result below.

_____
_____
_____
_____

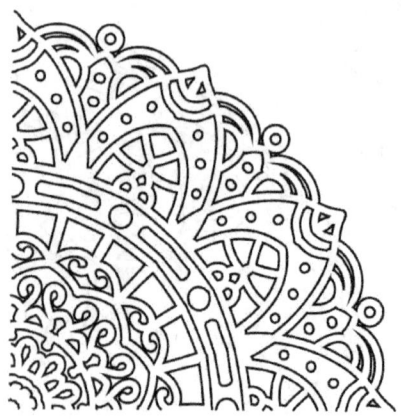
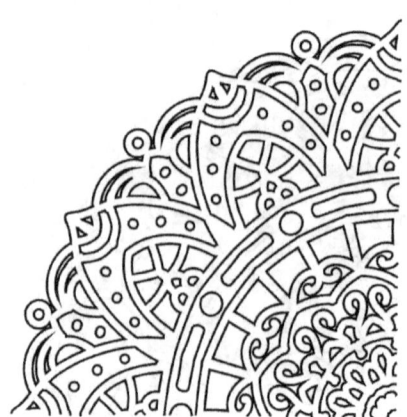

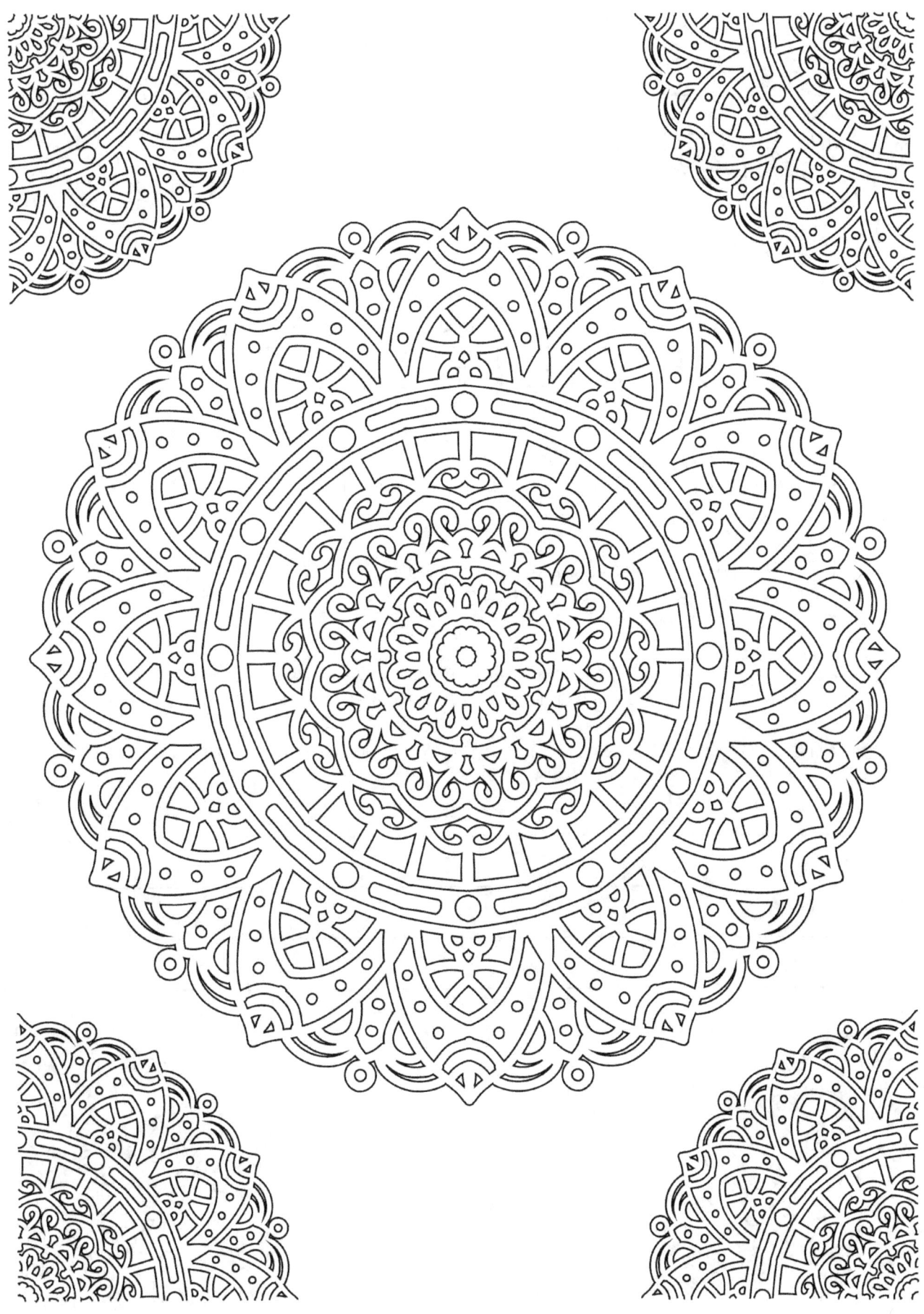

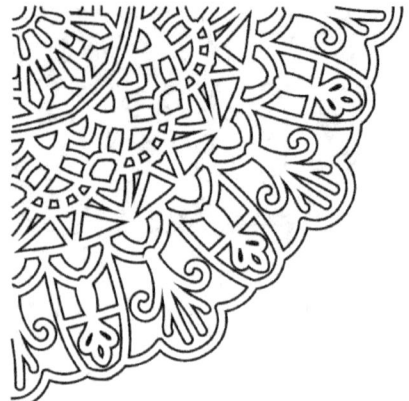
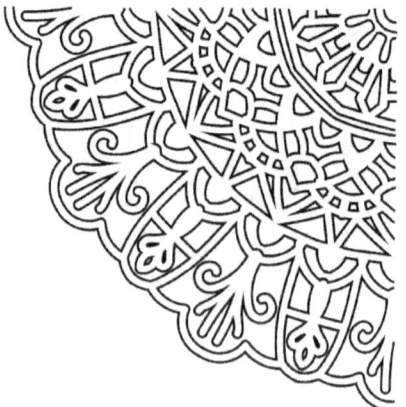

MANDALA #08

Coloring a mandala, is a great way to tune into our subconscious and see what emotional and mental state we are in.
These 3 steps will allow you to create a personal mandala:

1. Find a comfortable place to work. Sit in a quiet place where you won't be interrupted. Concentrate on the problem you want to solve the most in the moment.

2. Fill the shape with colors that reflect your current state of mind. Let your imagination run wild. There are no rules when creating a mandala.

3. Take some time to reflect on your mandala and what it means to you, and write down the result below.

_____
_____
_____
_____

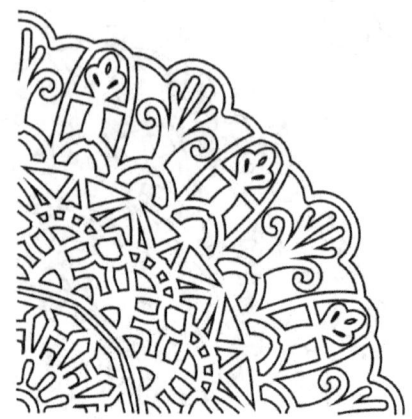
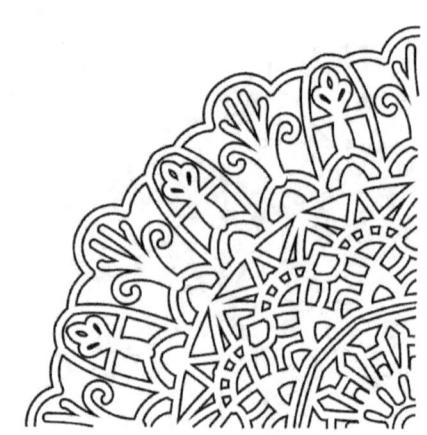

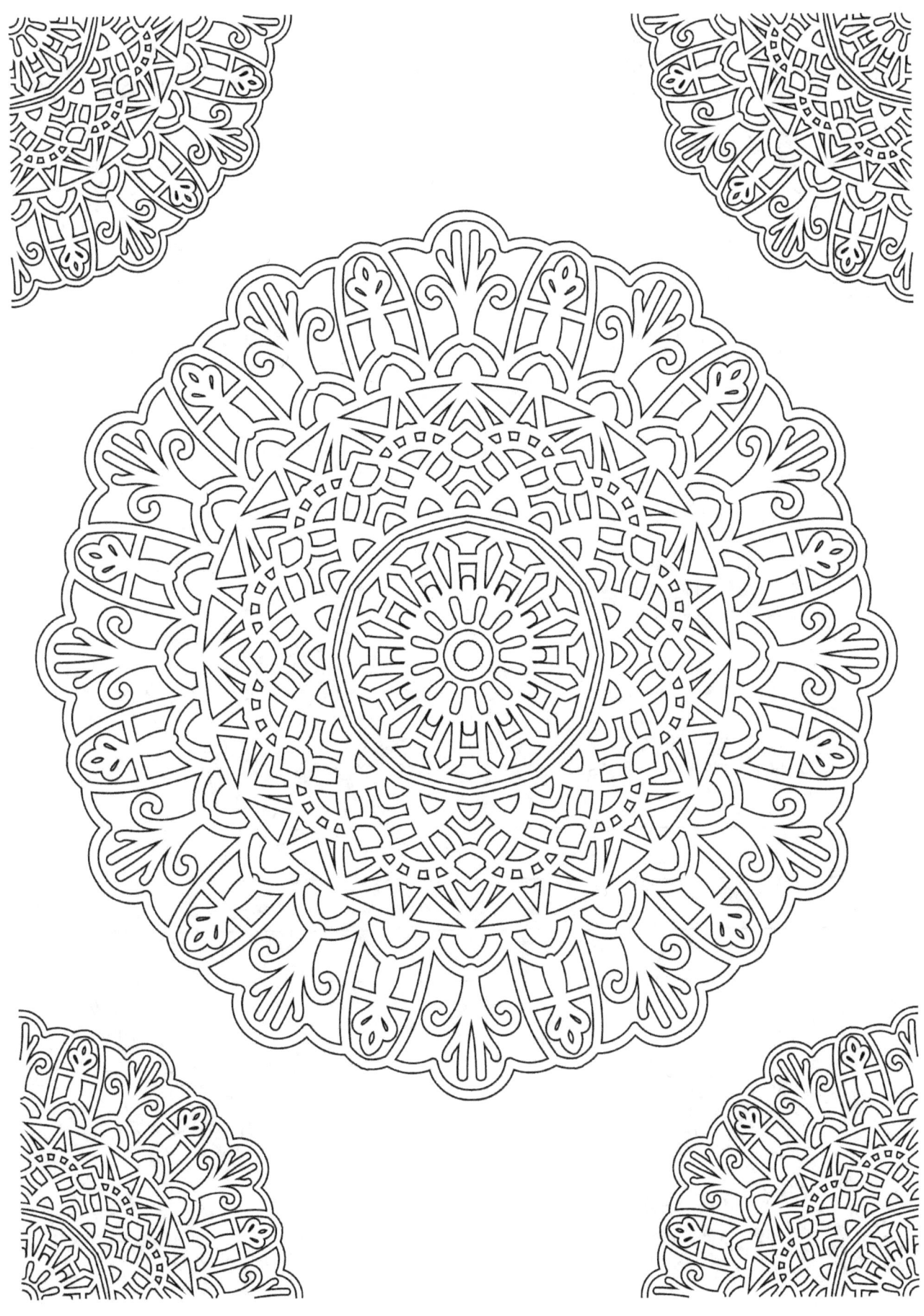

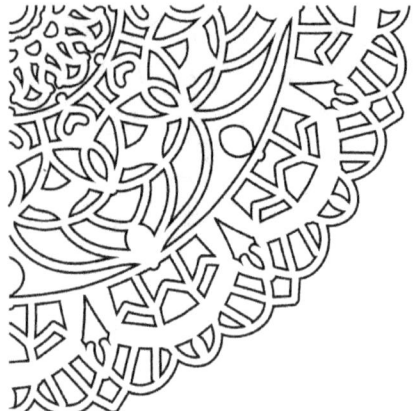
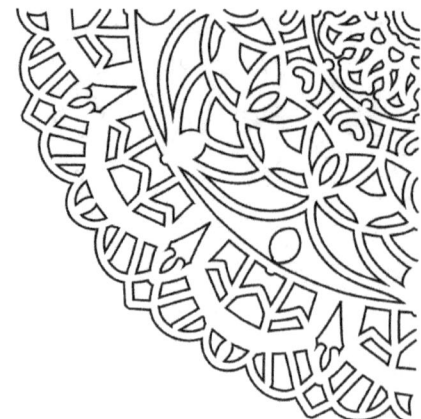

MANDALA #09

Coloring a mandala, is a great way to tune into our subconscious and see what emotional and mental state we are in.

These 3 steps will allow you to create a personal mandala:

1. Find a comfortable place to work. Sit in a quiet place where you won't be interrupted. Concentrate on the problem you want to solve the most in the moment.

2. Fill the shape with colors that reflect your current state of mind. Let your imagination run wild. There are no rules when creating a mandala.

3. Take some time to reflect on your mandala and what it means to you, and write down the result below.

_____
_____
_____
_____

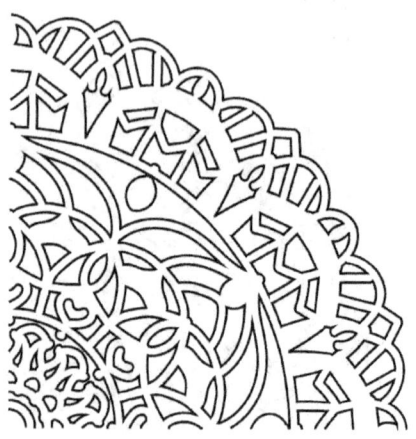
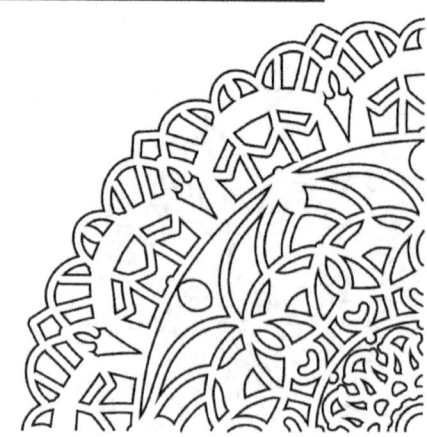

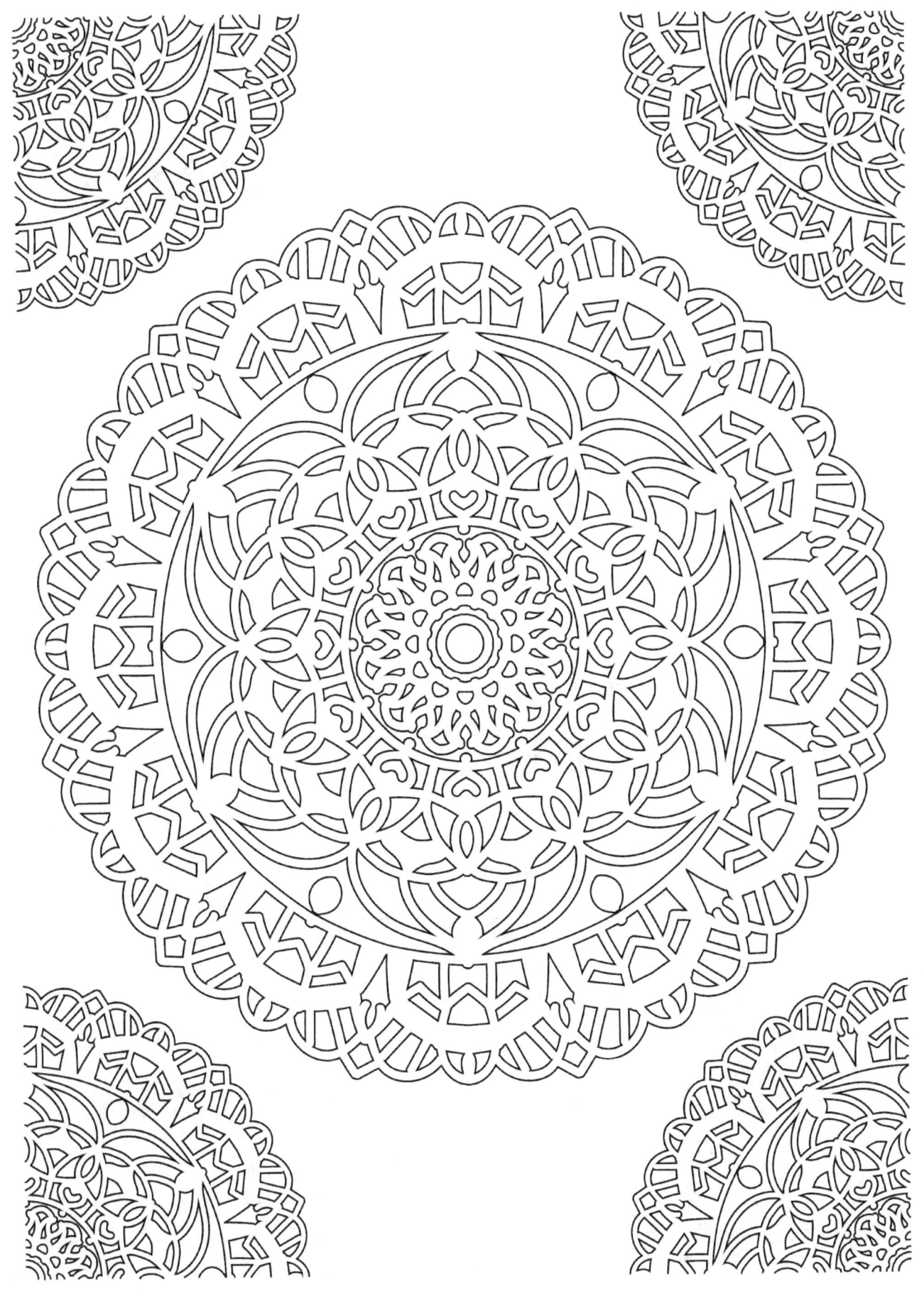

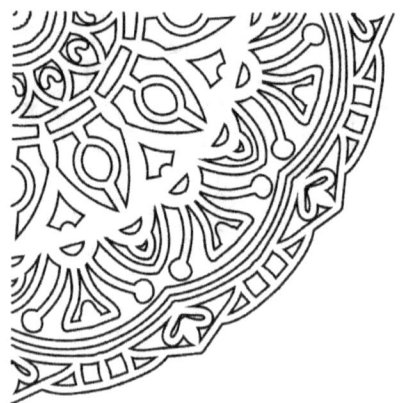
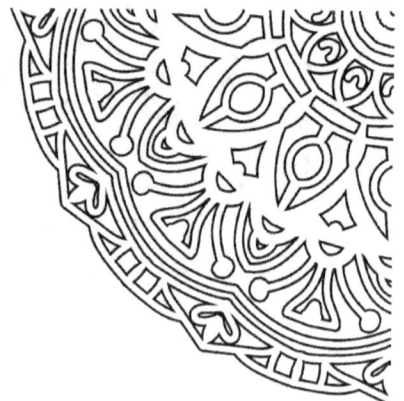

MANDALA #10

Coloring a mandala, is a great way to tune into our subconscious and see what emotional and mental state we are in.

These 3 steps will allow you to create a personal mandala:

1. Find a comfortable place to work. Sit in a quiet place where you won't be interrupted. Concentrate on the problem you want to solve the most in the moment.

2. Fill the shape with colors that reflect your current state of mind. Let your imagination run wild. There are no rules when creating a mandala.

3. Take some time to reflect on your mandala and what it means to you, and write down the result below.

_____

_____

_____

_____

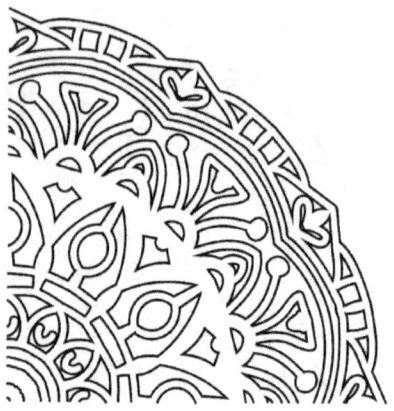
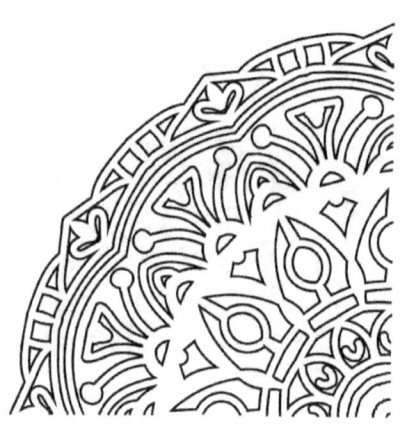

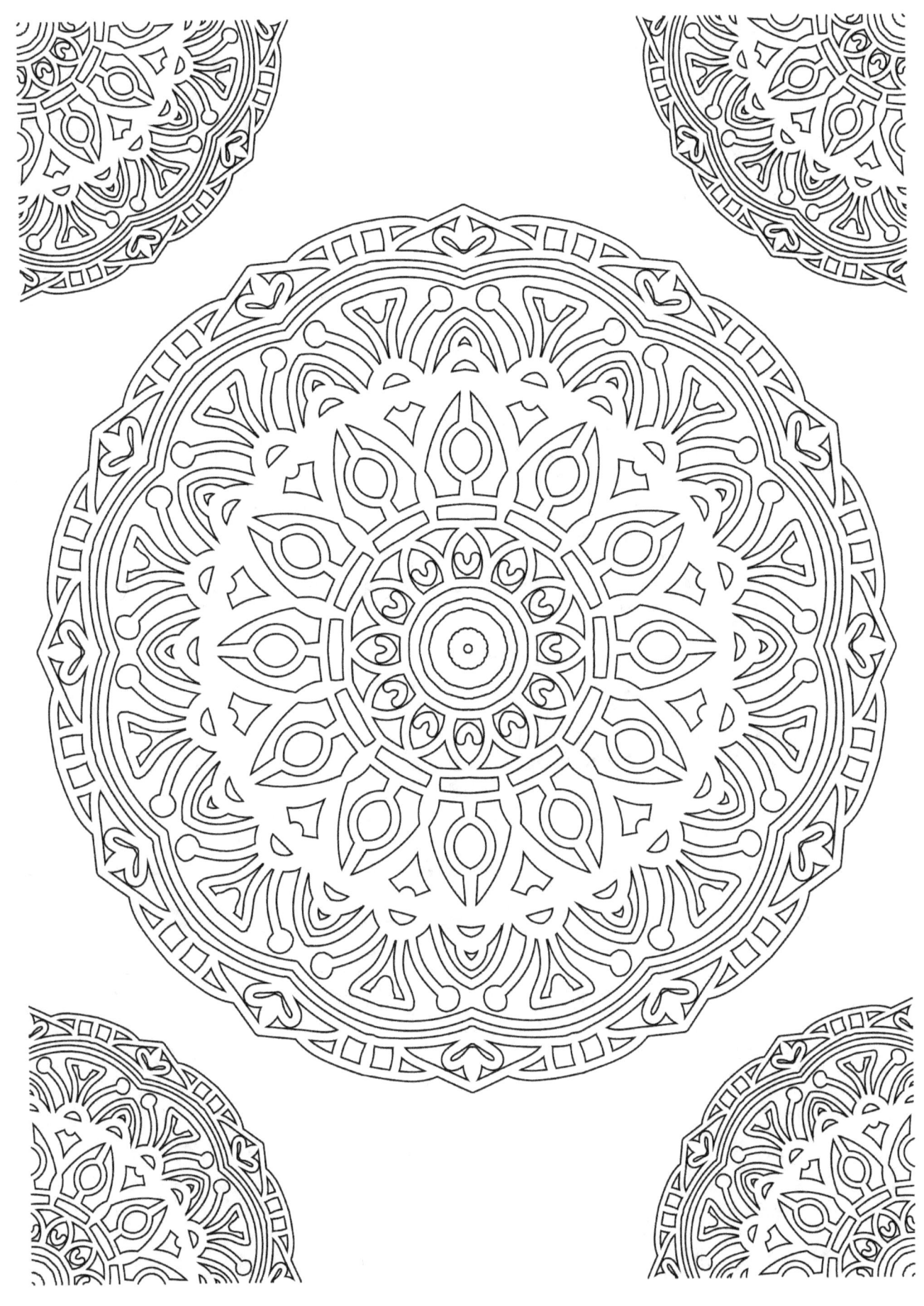

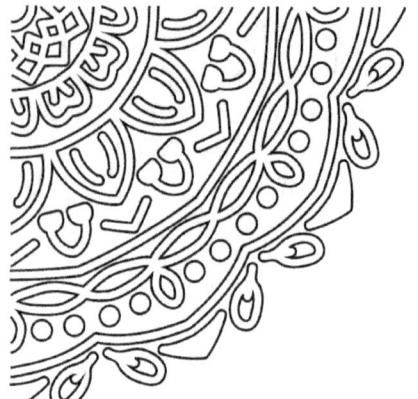
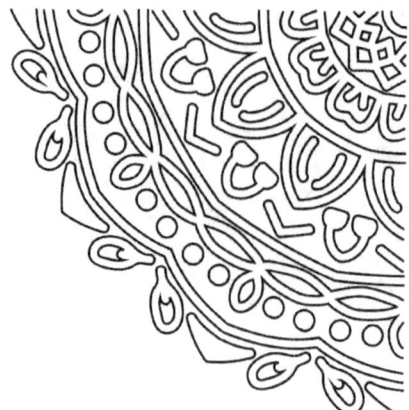

MANDALA #11

Coloring a mandala, is a great way to tune into our subconscious and see what emotional and mental state we are in.

These 3 steps will allow you to create a personal mandala:

1. Find a comfortable place to work. Sit in a quiet place where you won't be interrupted. Concentrate on the problem you want to solve the most in the moment.

2. Fill the shape with colors that reflect your current state of mind. Let your imagination run wild. There are no rules when creating a mandala.

3. Take some time to reflect on your mandala and what it means to you, and write down the result below.

_____
_____
_____
_____

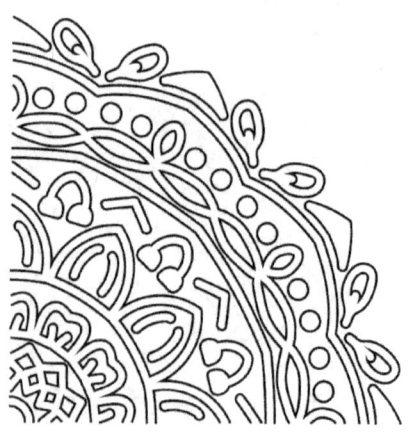
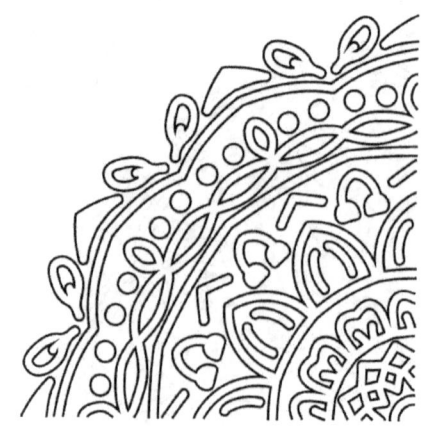

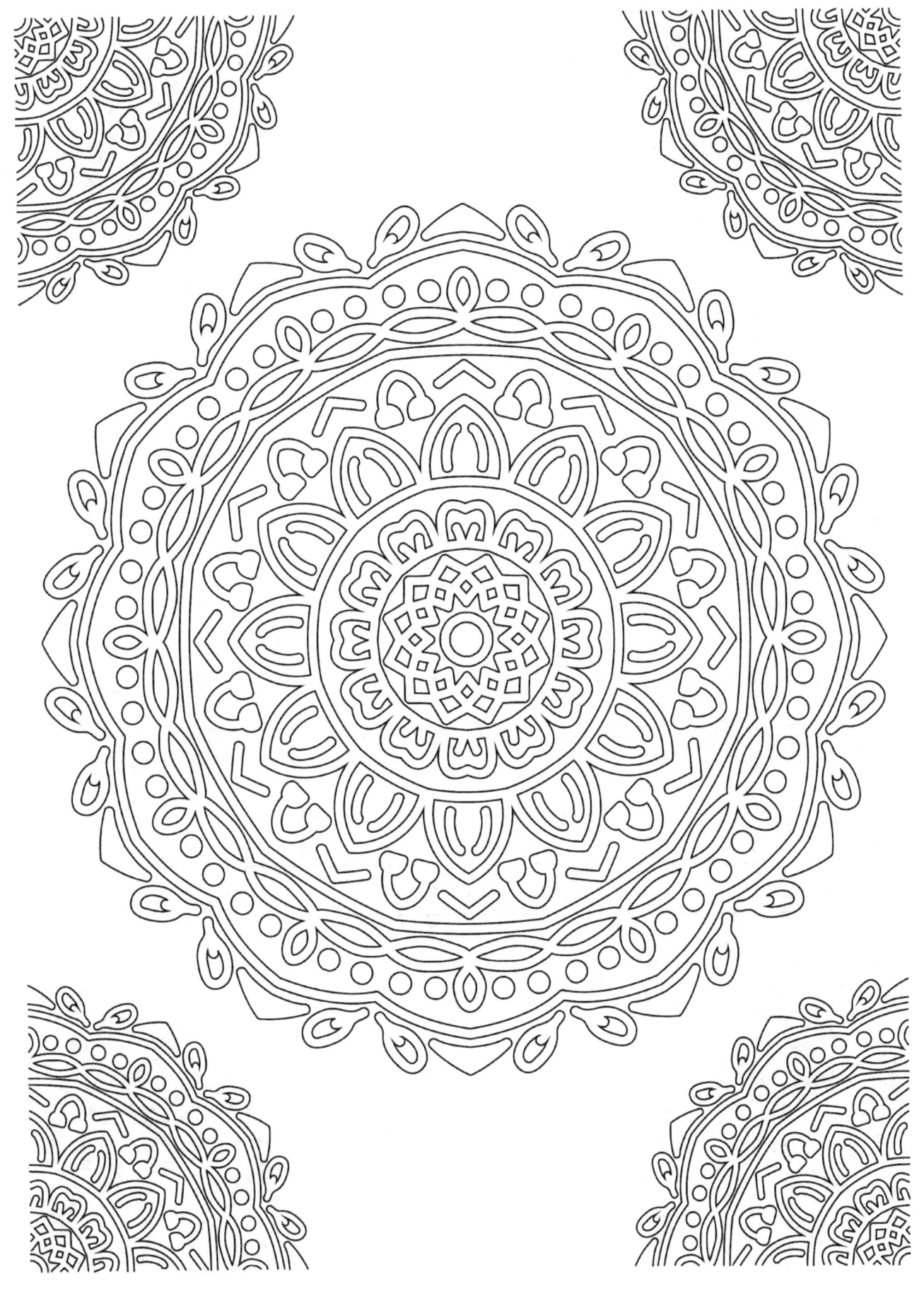

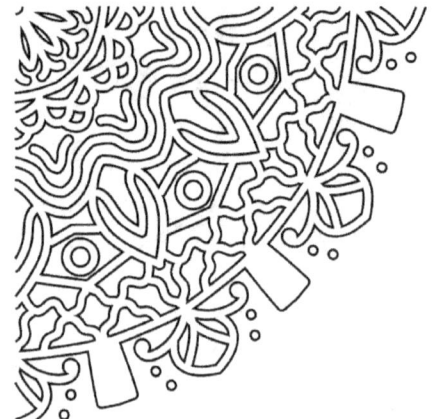
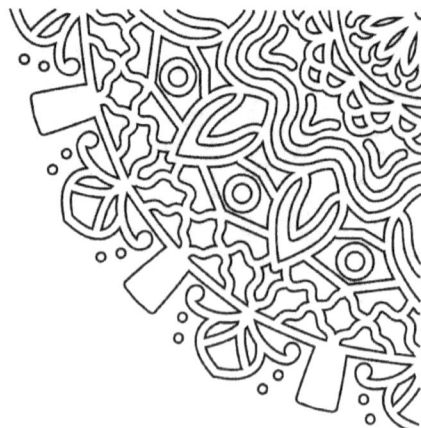

MANDALA #12

Coloring a mandala, is a great way to tune into our subconscious and see what emotional and mental state we are in.
These 3 steps will allow you to create a personal mandala:

1. Find a comfortable place to work. Sit in a quiet place where you won't be interrupted. Concentrate on the problem you want to solve the most in the moment.

2. Fill the shape with colors that reflect your current state of mind. Let your imagination run wild. There are no rules when creating a mandala.

3. Take some time to reflect on your mandala and what it means to you, and write down the result below.

_____
_____
_____
_____

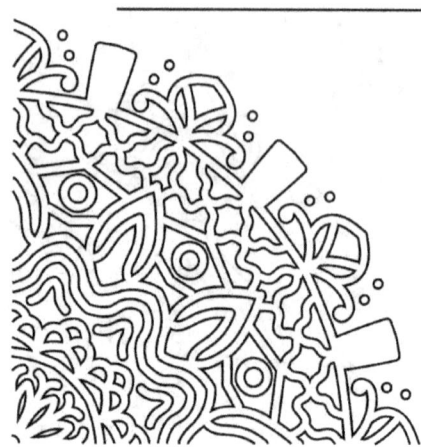
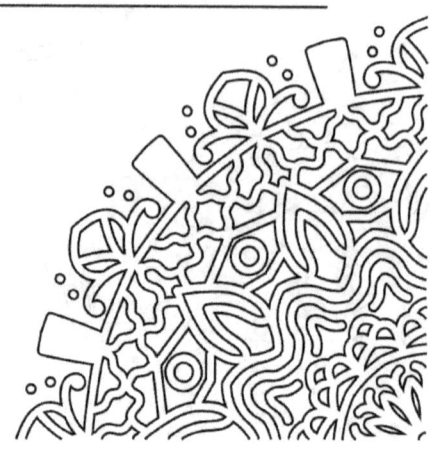

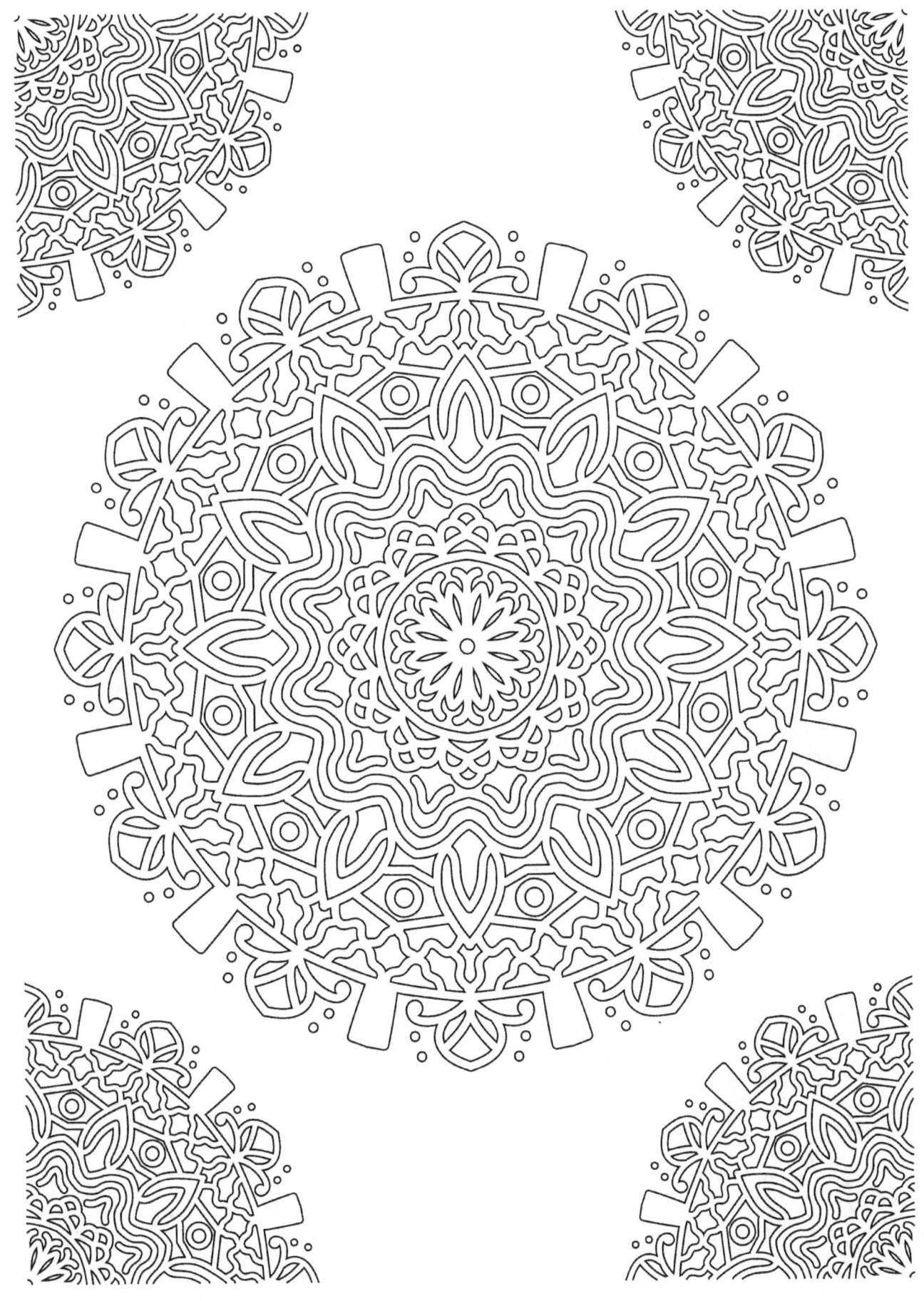

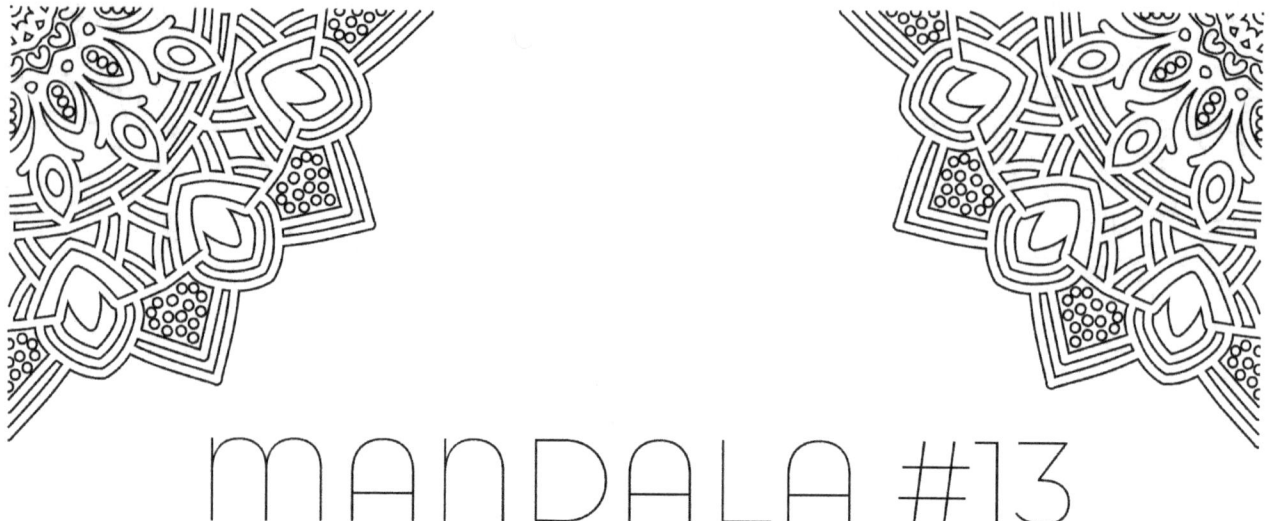

MANDALA #13

Coloring a mandala, is a great way to tune into our subconscious and see what emotional and mental state we are in.

These 3 steps will allow you to create a personal mandala:

1. Find a comfortable place to work. Sit in a quiet place where you won't be interrupted. Concentrate on the problem you want to solve the most in the moment.

2. Fill the shape with colors that reflect your current state of mind. Let your imagination run wild. There are no rules when creating a mandala.

3. Take some time to reflect on your mandala and what it means to you, and write down the result below.

_____

_____

_____

_____

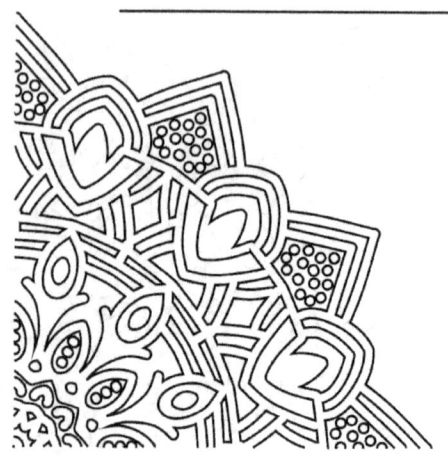
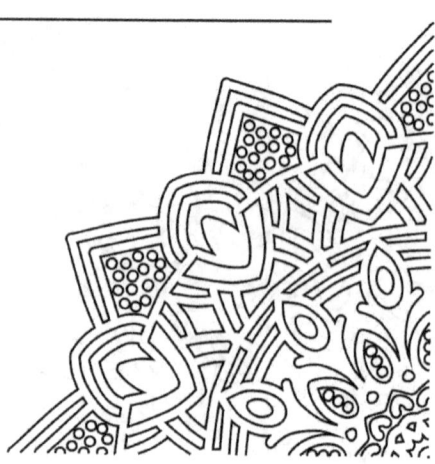

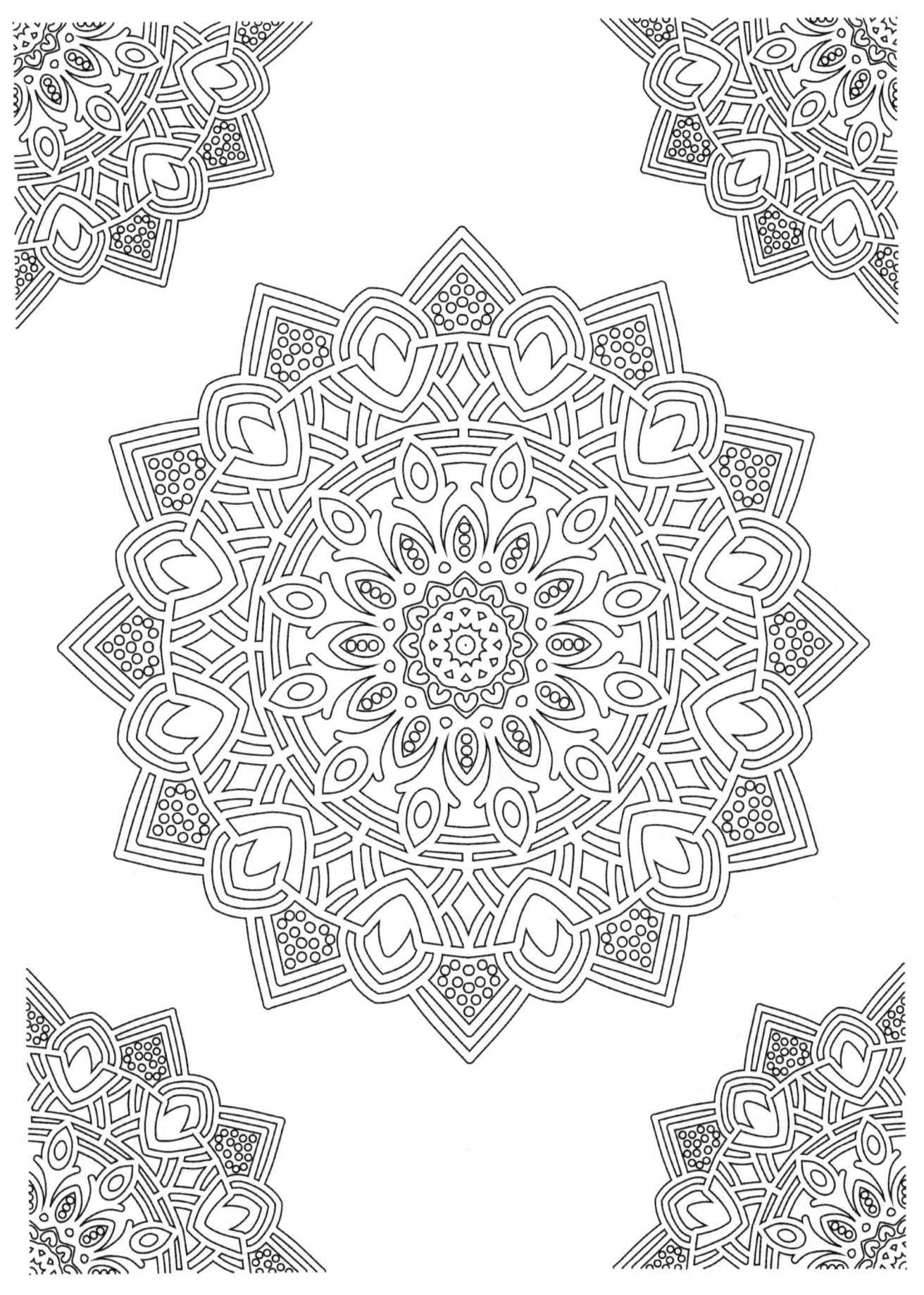

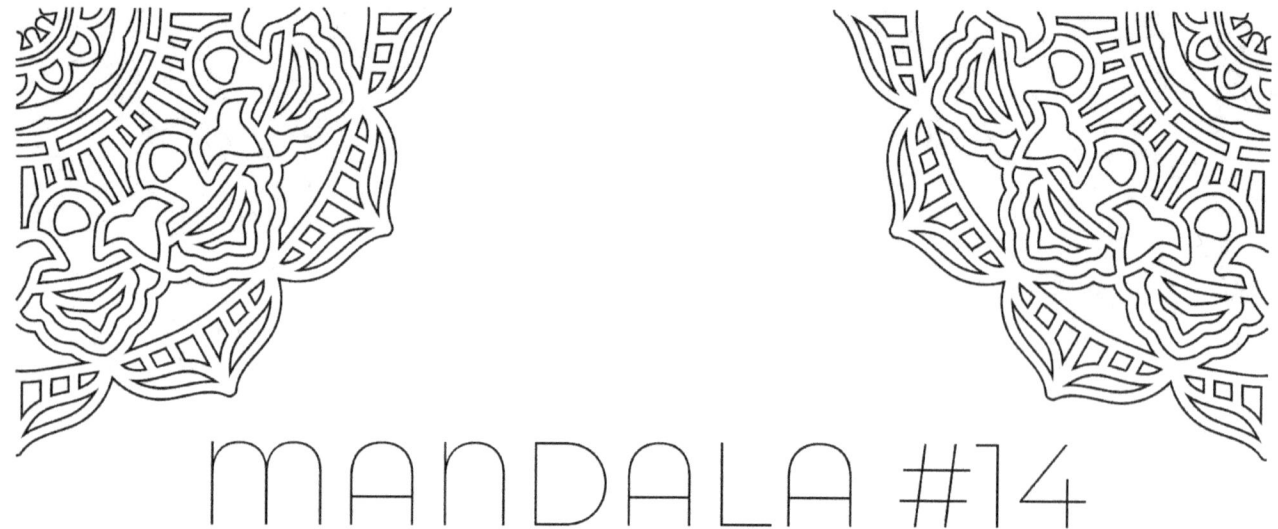

MANDALA #14

Coloring a mandala, is a great way to tune into our subconscious and see what emotional and mental state we are in.
These 3 steps will allow you to create a personal mandala:

1. Find a comfortable place to work. Sit in a quiet place where you won't be interrupted. Concentrate on the problem you want to solve the most in the moment.

2. Fill the shape with colors that reflect your current state of mind. Let your imagination run wild. There are no rules when creating a mandala.

3. Take some time to reflect on your mandala and what it means to you, and write down the result below.

_____

_____

_____

_____

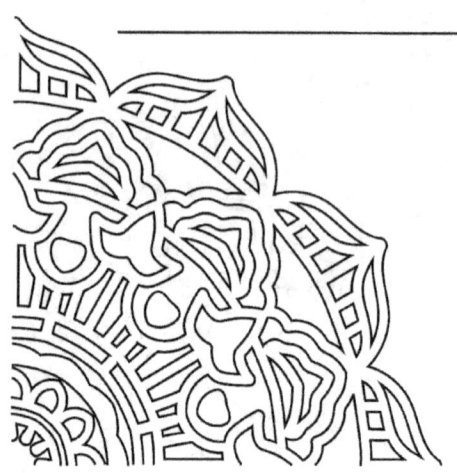
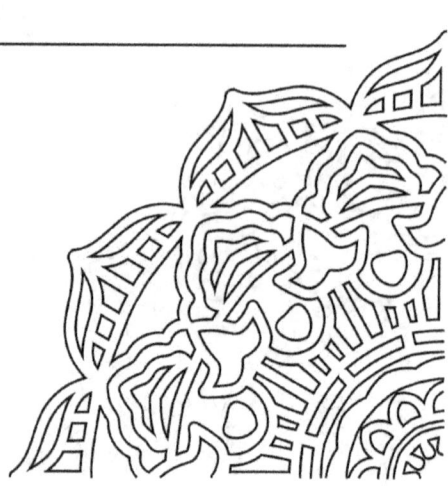

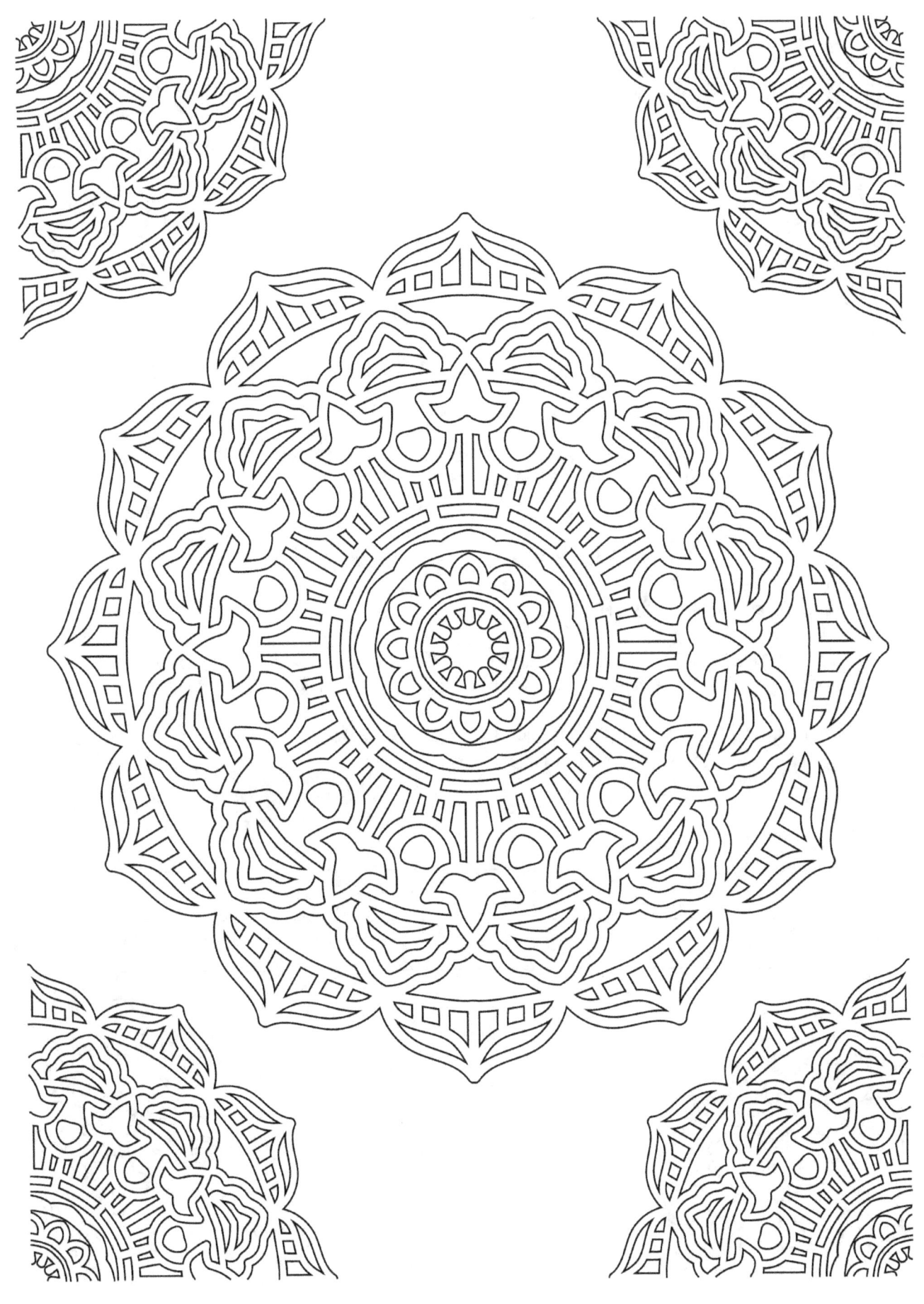

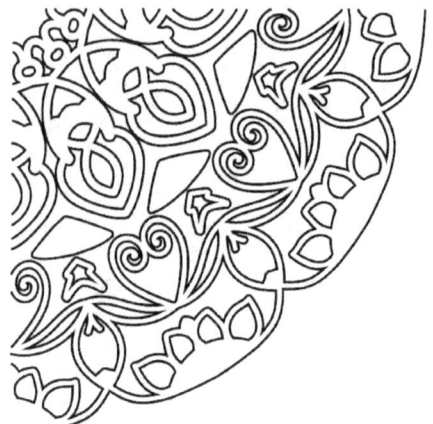
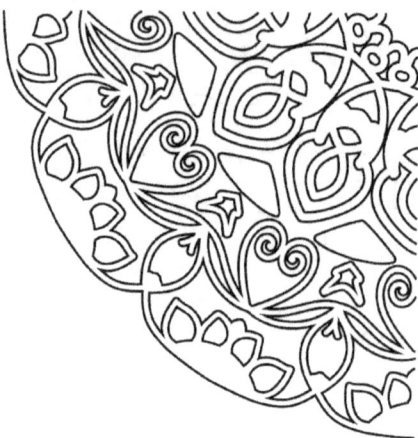

MANDALA #15

Coloring a mandala, is a great way to tune into our subconscious and see what emotional and mental state we are in.

These 3 steps will allow you to create a personal mandala:

1. Find a comfortable place to work. Sit in a quiet place where you won't be interrupted. Concentrate on the problem you want to solve the most in the moment.

2. Fill the shape with colors that reflect your current state of mind. Let your imagination run wild. There are no rules when creating a mandala.

3. Take some time to reflect on your mandala and what it means to you, and write down the result below.

_____
_____
_____
_____

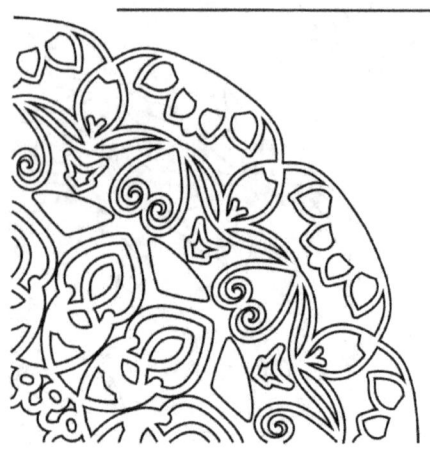
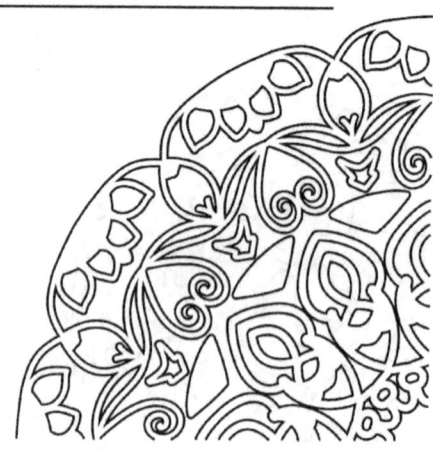

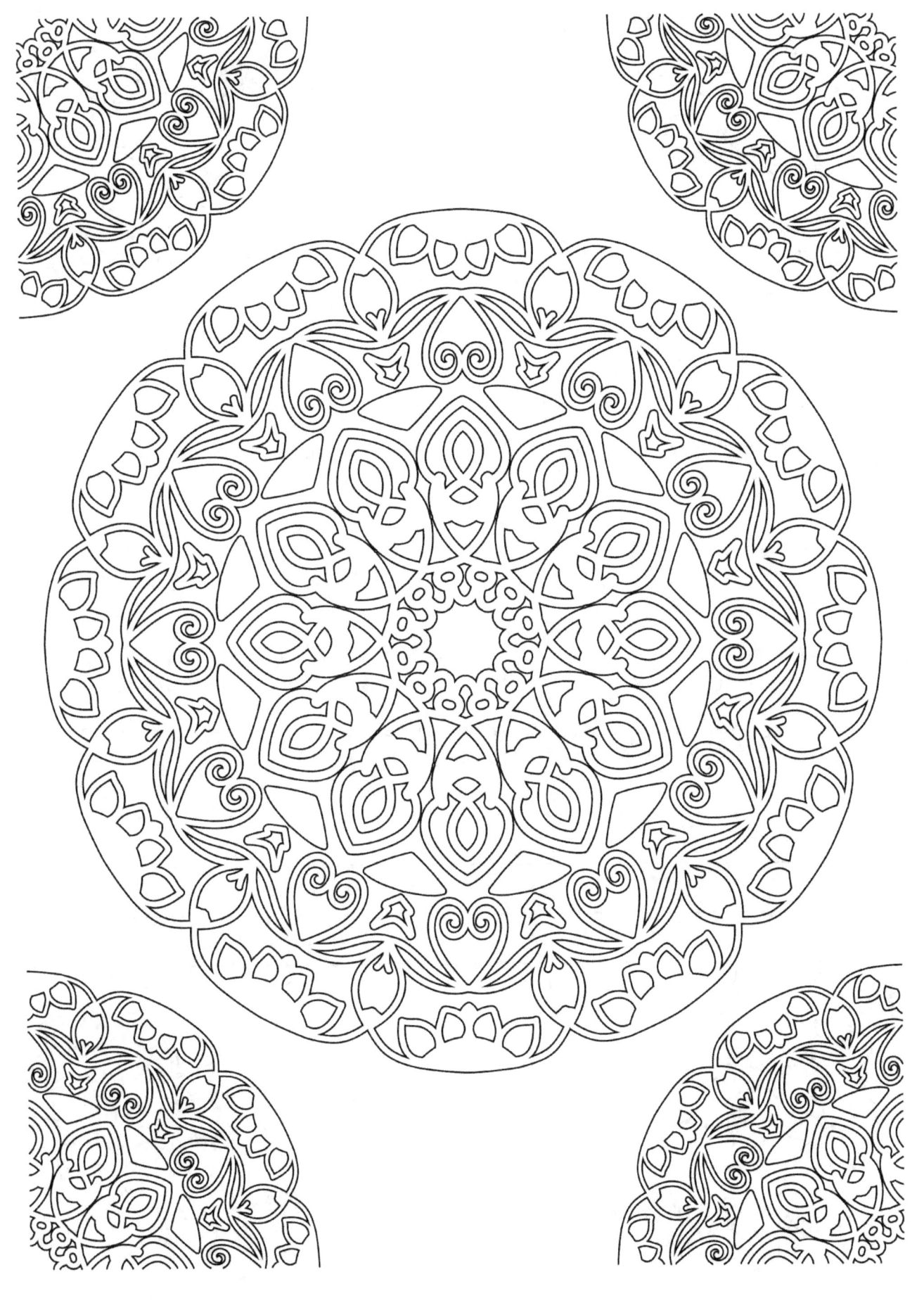

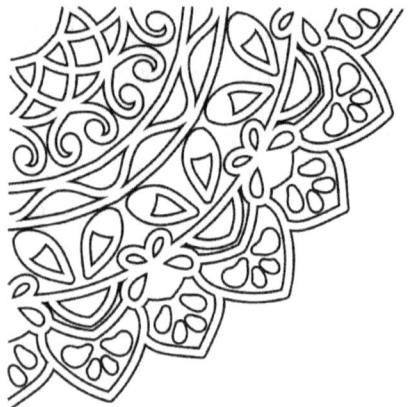
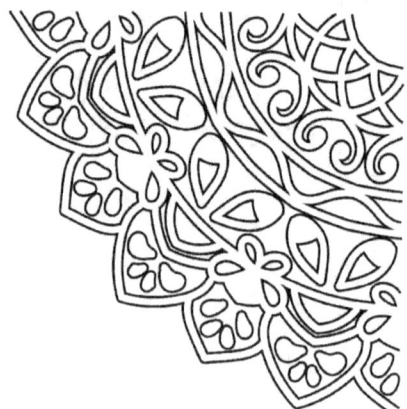

MANDALA #16

Coloring a mandala, is a great way to tune into our subconscious and see what emotional and mental state we are in.
These 3 steps will allow you to create a personal mandala:

1. Find a comfortable place to work. Sit in a quiet place where you won't be interrupted. Concentrate on the problem you want to solve the most in the moment.

2. Fill the shape with colors that reflect your current state of mind. Let your imagination run wild. There are no rules when creating a mandala.

3. Take some time to reflect on your mandala and what it means to you, and write down the result below.

_____
_____
_____
_____

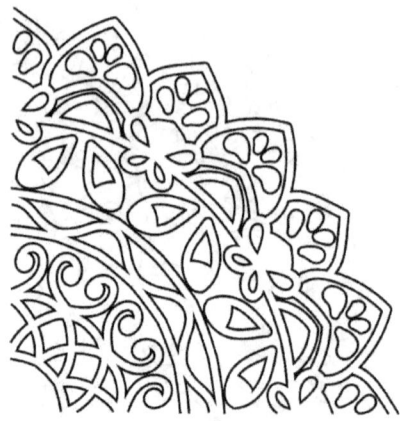
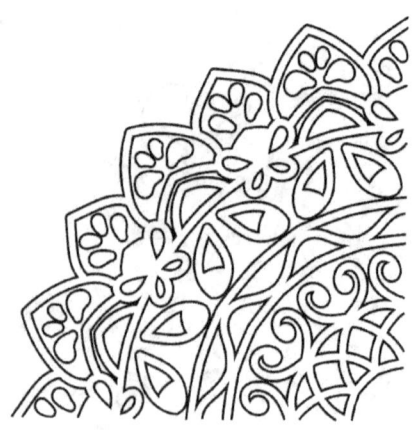

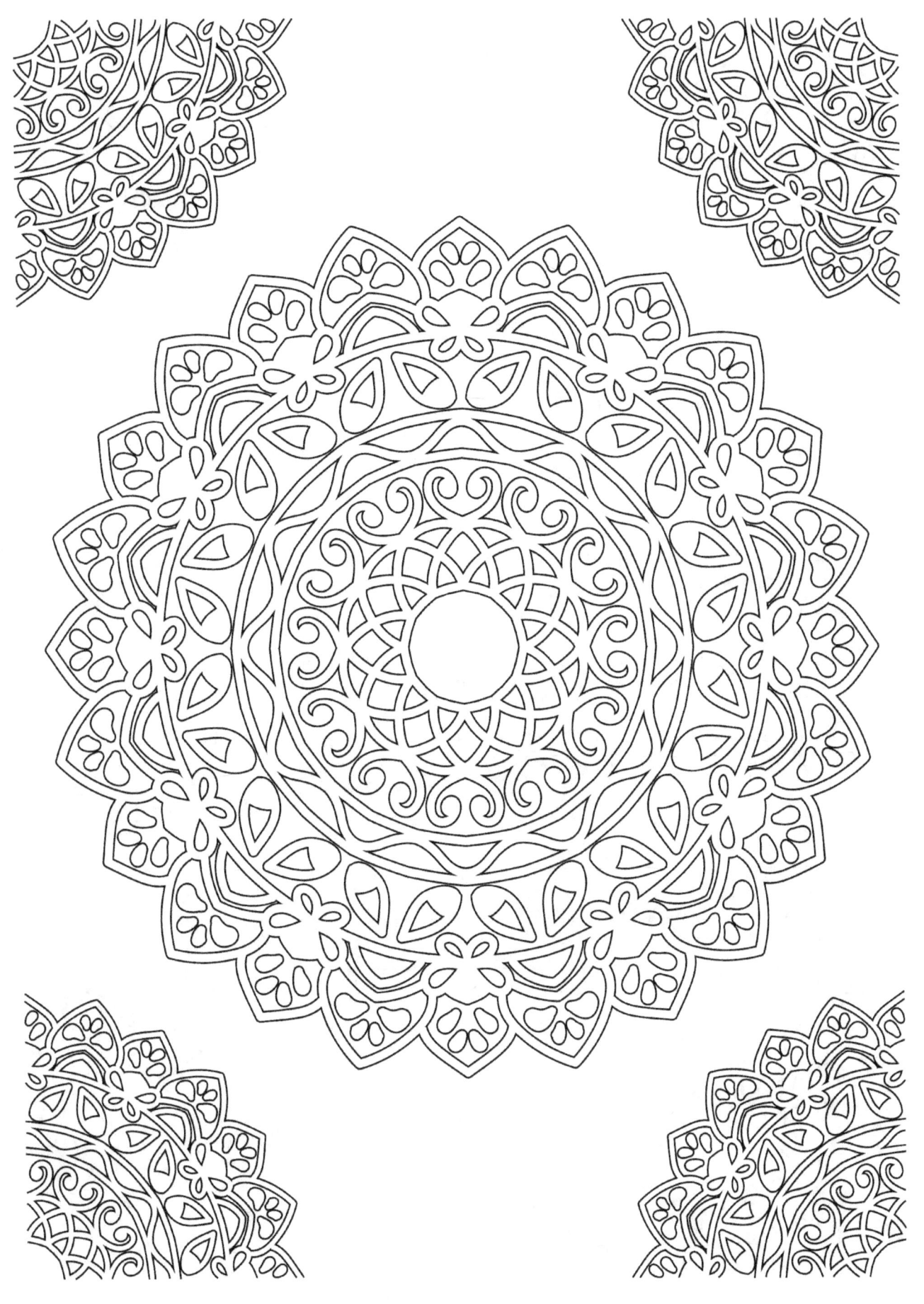

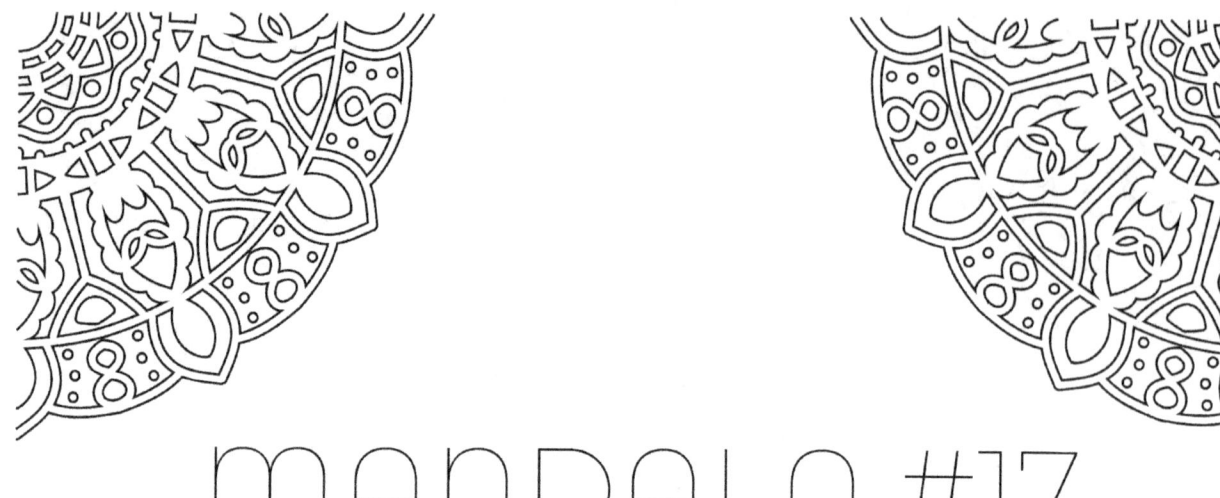

MANDALA #17

Coloring a mandala, is a great way to tune into our subconscious and see what emotional and mental state we are in.

These 3 steps will allow you to create a personal mandala:

1. Find a comfortable place to work. Sit in a quiet place where you won't be interrupted. Concentrate on the problem you want to solve the most in the moment.

2. Fill the shape with colors that reflect your current state of mind. Let your imagination run wild. There are no rules when creating a mandala.

3. Take some time to reflect on your mandala and what it means to you, and write down the result below.

_____
_____
_____
_____

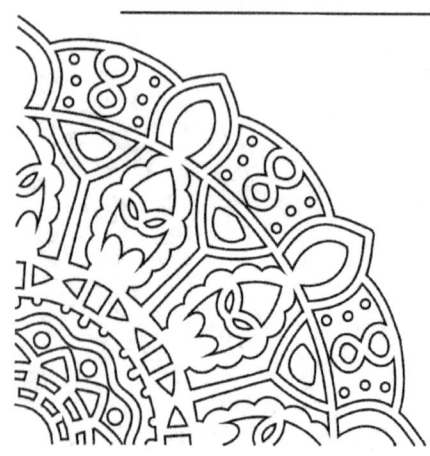
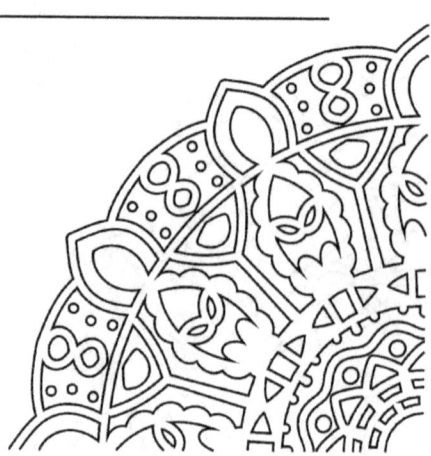

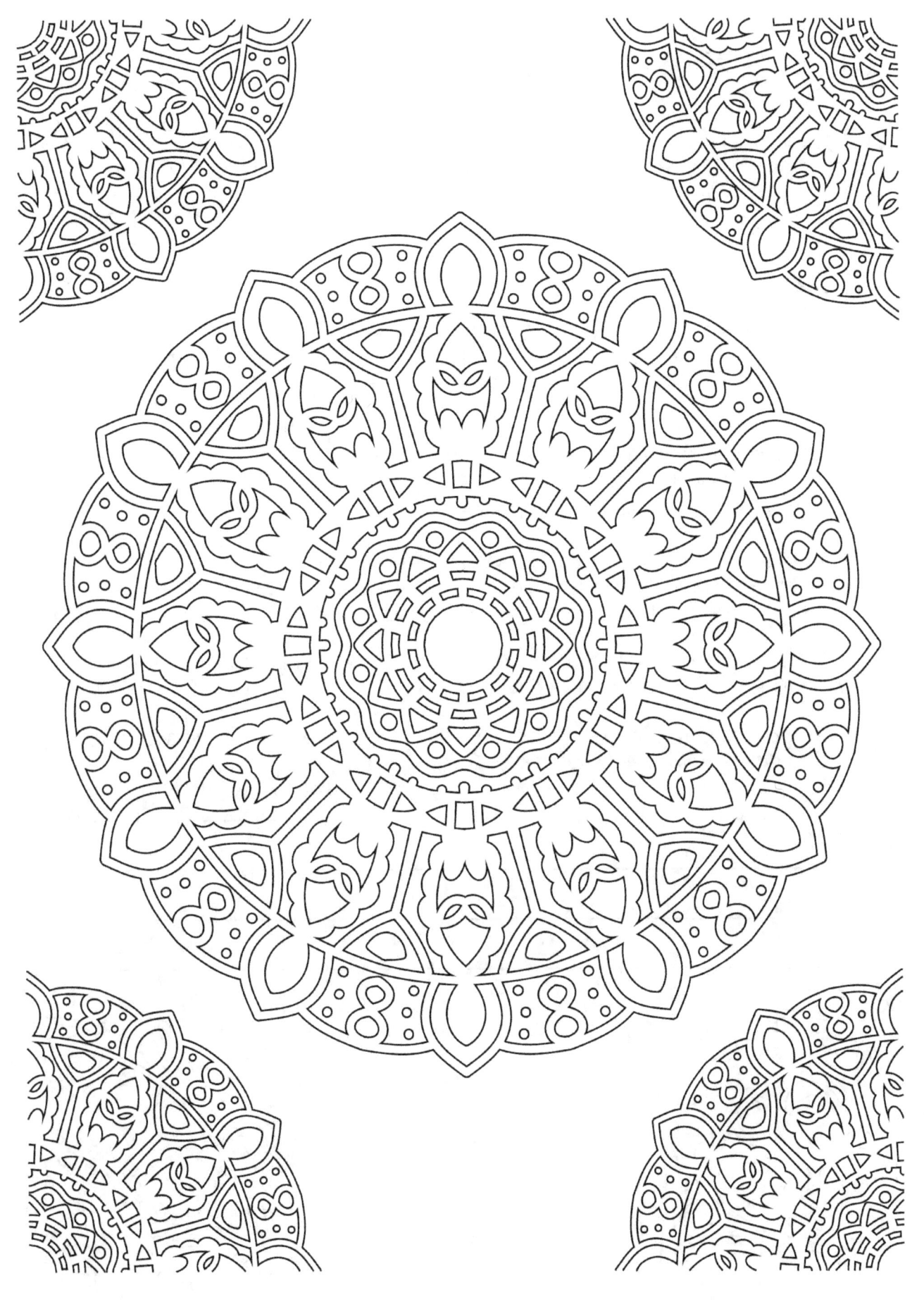

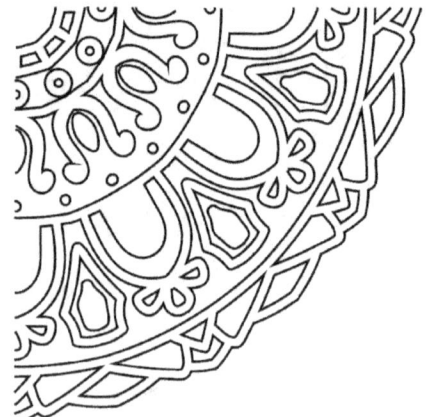
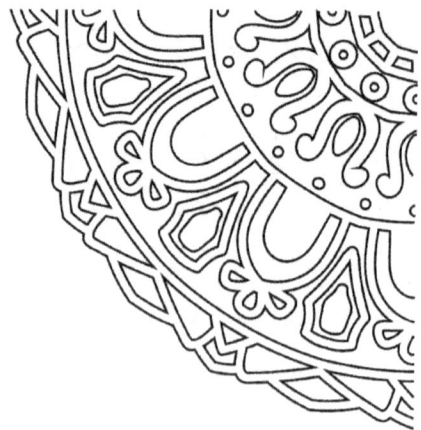

MANDALA #18

Coloring a mandala, is a great way to tune into our subconscious and see what emotional and mental state we are in.
These 3 steps will allow you to create a personal mandala:

1. Find a comfortable place to work. Sit in a quiet place where you won't be interrupted. Concentrate on the problem you want to solve the most in the moment.

2. Fill the shape with colors that reflect your current state of mind. Let your imagination run wild. There are no rules when creating a mandala.

3. Take some time to reflect on your mandala and what it means to you, and write down the result below.

_____
_____
_____
_____

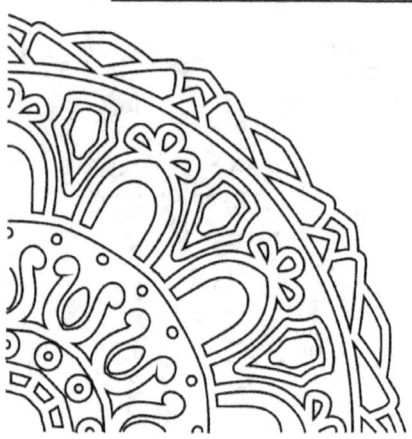
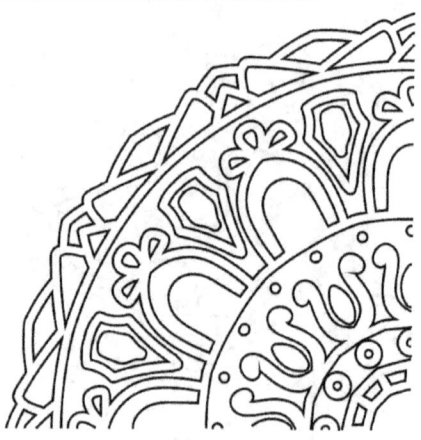

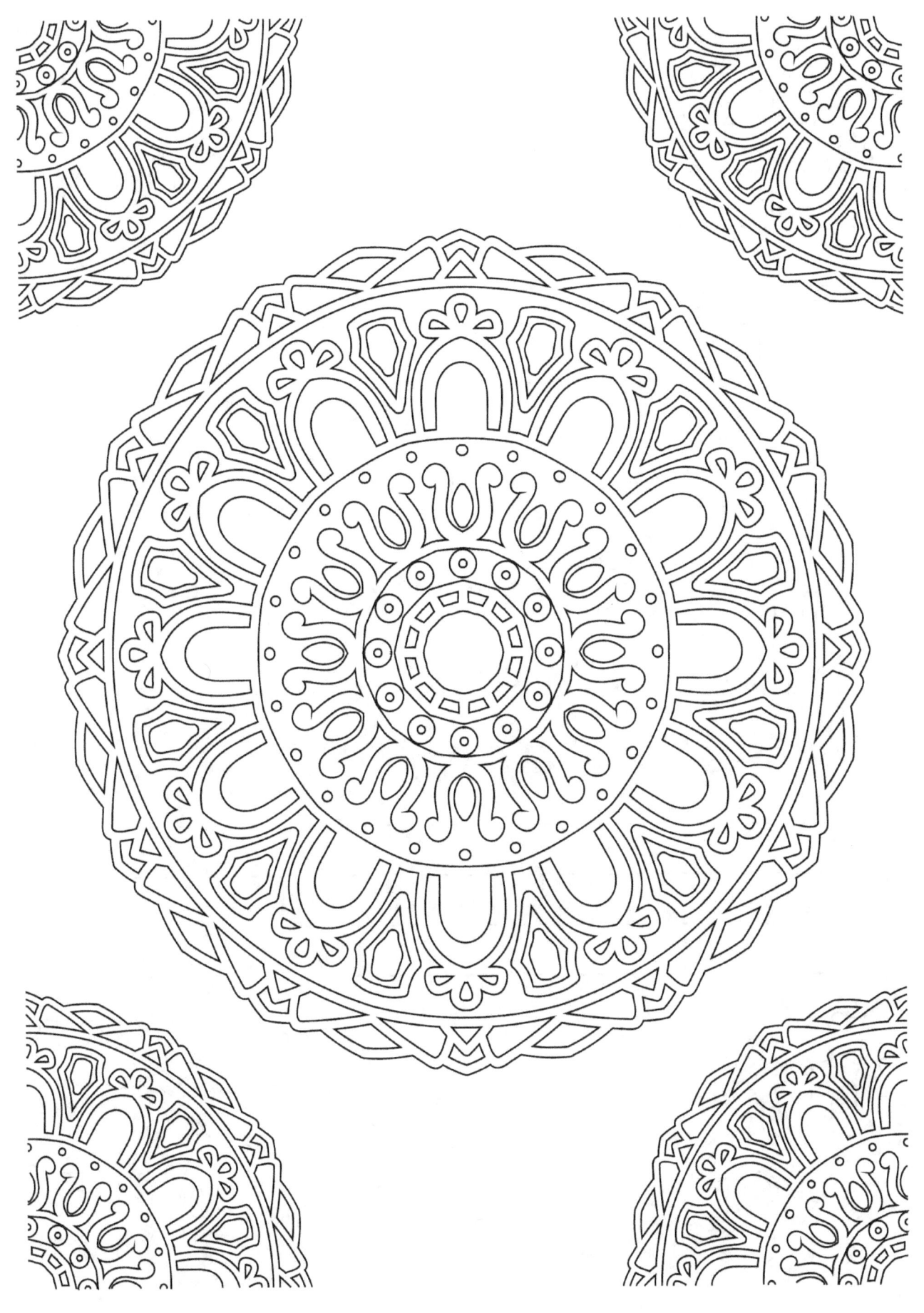

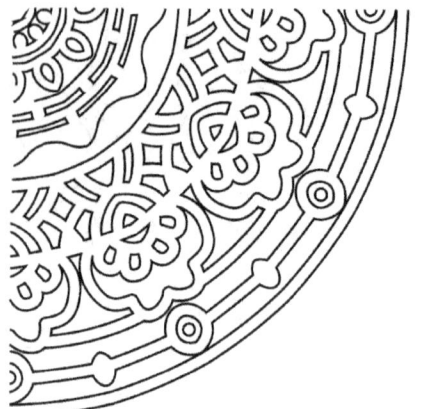 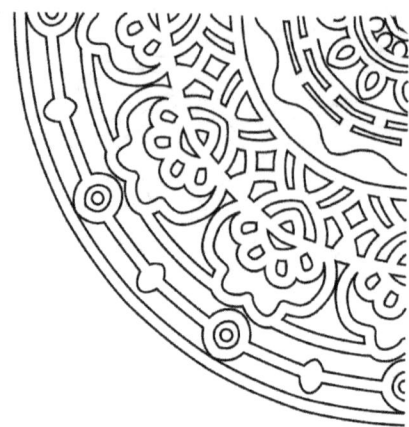

MANDALA #19

Coloring a mandala, is a great way to tune into our subconscious and see what emotional and mental state we are in.

These 3 steps will allow you to create a personal mandala:

1. Find a comfortable place to work. Sit in a quiet place where you won't be interrupted. Concentrate on the problem you want to solve the most in the moment.

2. Fill the shape with colors that reflect your current state of mind. Let your imagination run wild. There are no rules when creating a mandala.

3. Take some time to reflect on your mandala and what it means to you, and write down the result below.

_____

_____

_____

_____

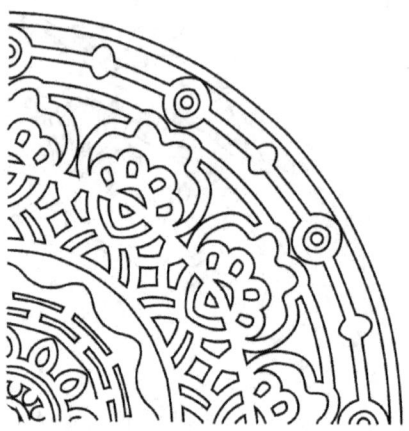 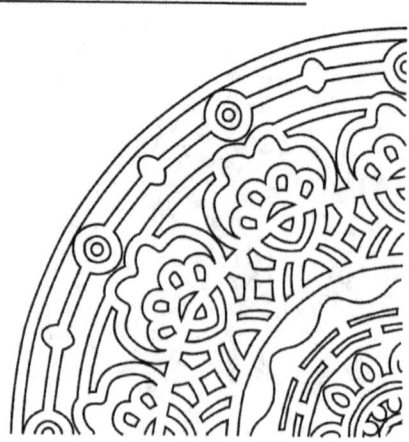

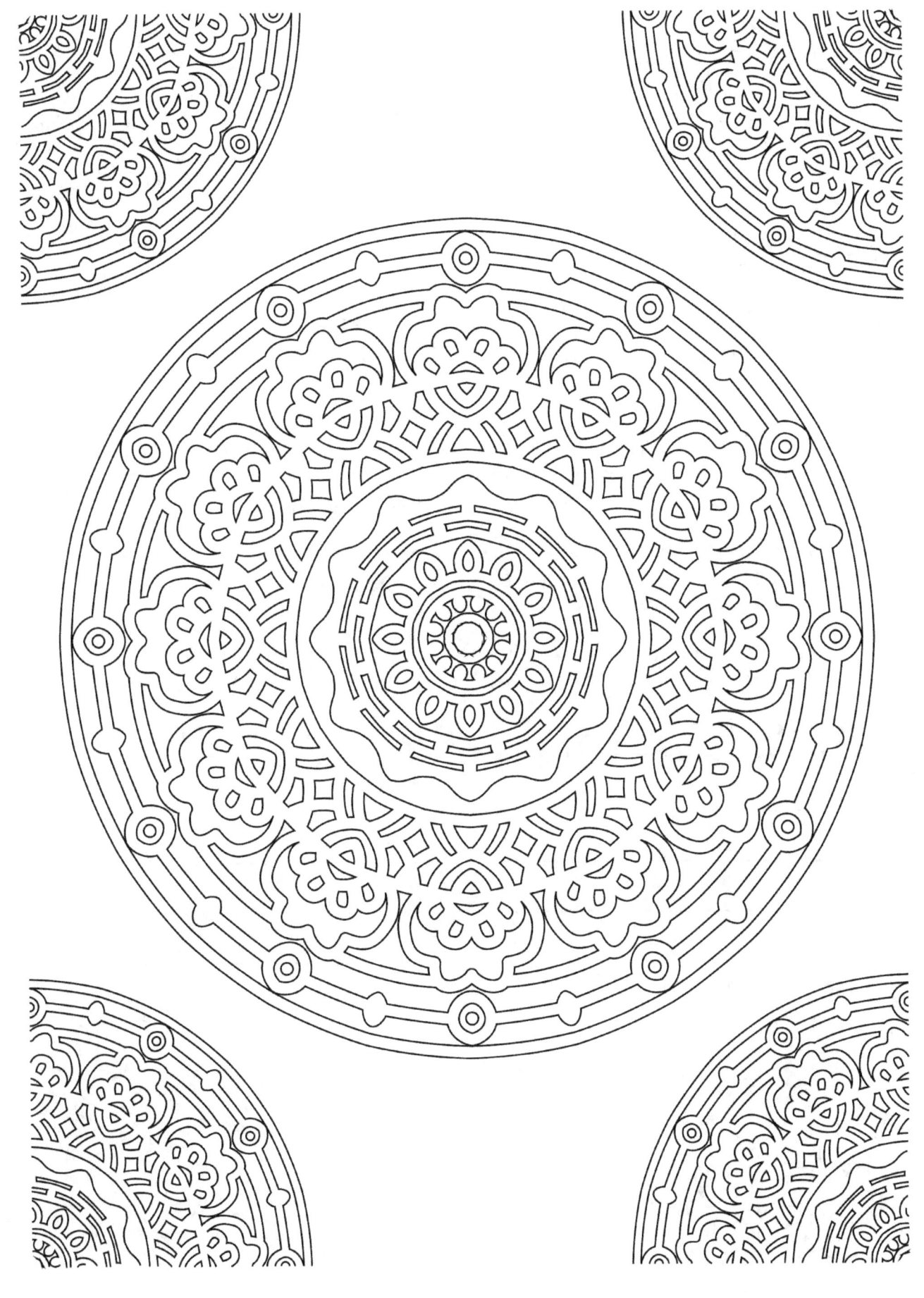

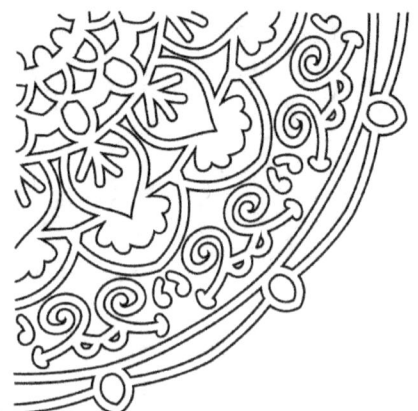 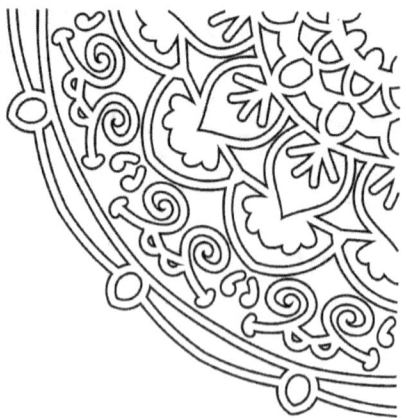

MANDALA #20

Coloring a mandala, is a great way to tune into our subconscious and see what emotional and mental state we are in.
These 3 steps will allow you to create a personal mandala:

1. Find a comfortable place to work. Sit in a quiet place where you won't be interrupted. Concentrate on the problem you want to solve the most in the moment.

2. Fill the shape with colors that reflect your current state of mind. Let your imagination run wild. There are no rules when creating a mandala.

3. Take some time to reflect on your mandala and what it means to you, and write down the result below.

_____
_____
_____
_____

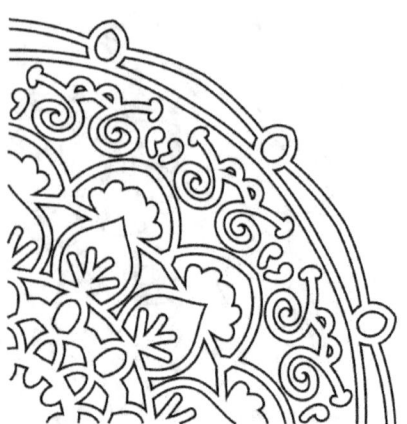 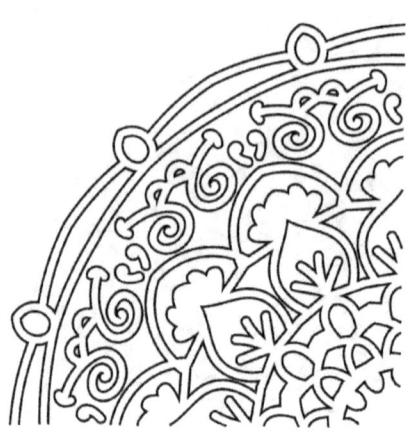

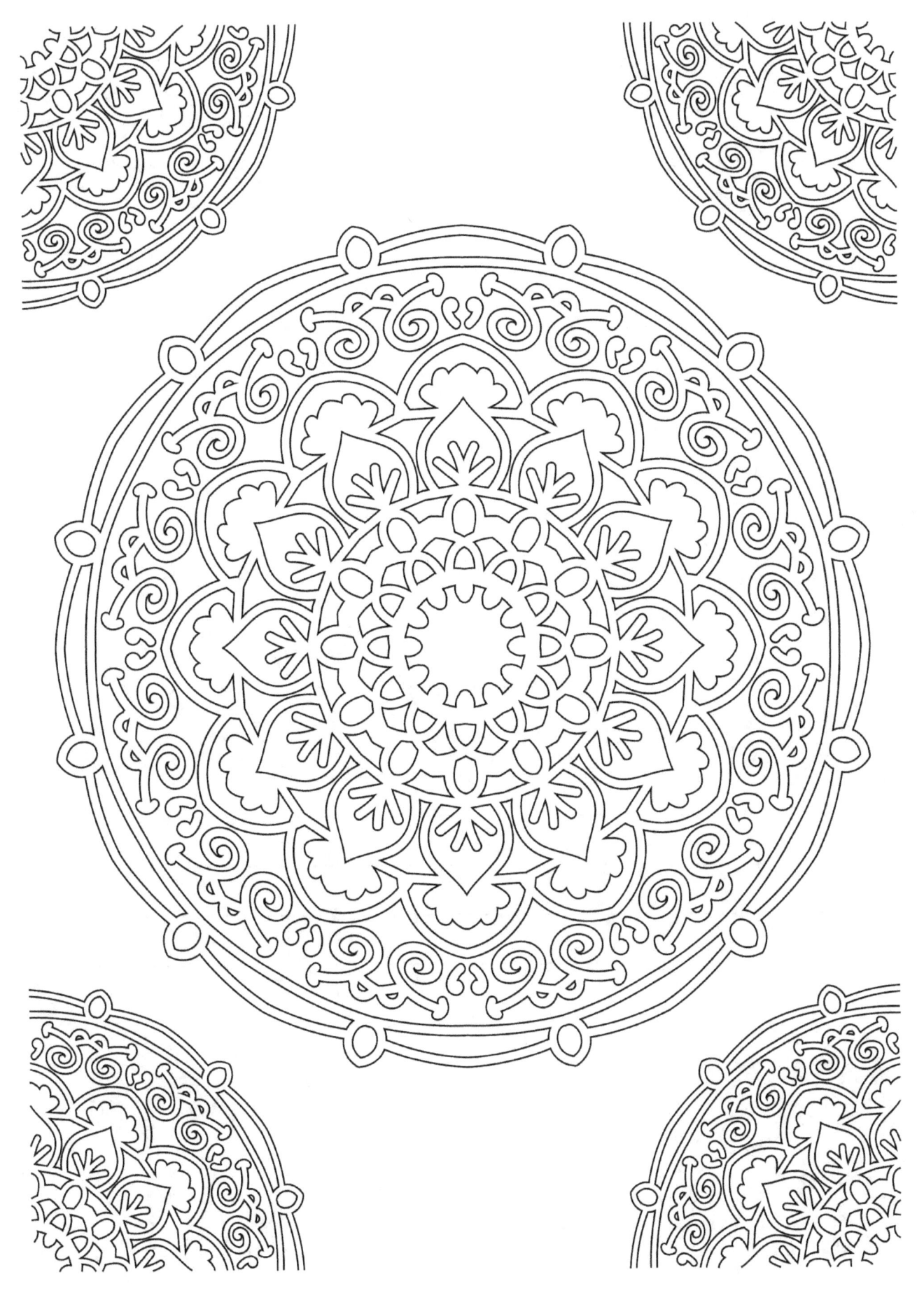

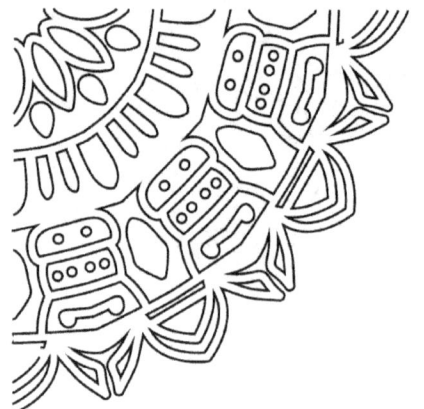
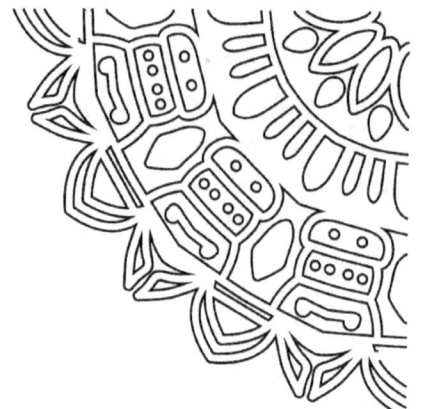

MANDALA #21

Coloring a mandala, is a great way to tune into our subconscious and see what emotional and mental state we are in.

These 3 steps will allow you to create a personal mandala:

1. Find a comfortable place to work. Sit in a quiet place where you won't be interrupted. Concentrate on the problem you want to solve the most in the moment.

2. Fill the shape with colors that reflect your current state of mind. Let your imagination run wild. There are no rules when creating a mandala.

3. Take some time to reflect on your mandala and what it means to you, and write down the result below.

_____

_____

_____

_____

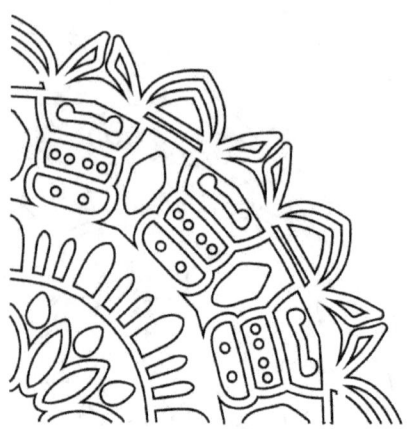
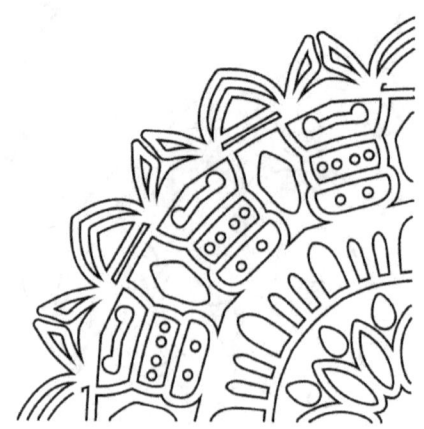

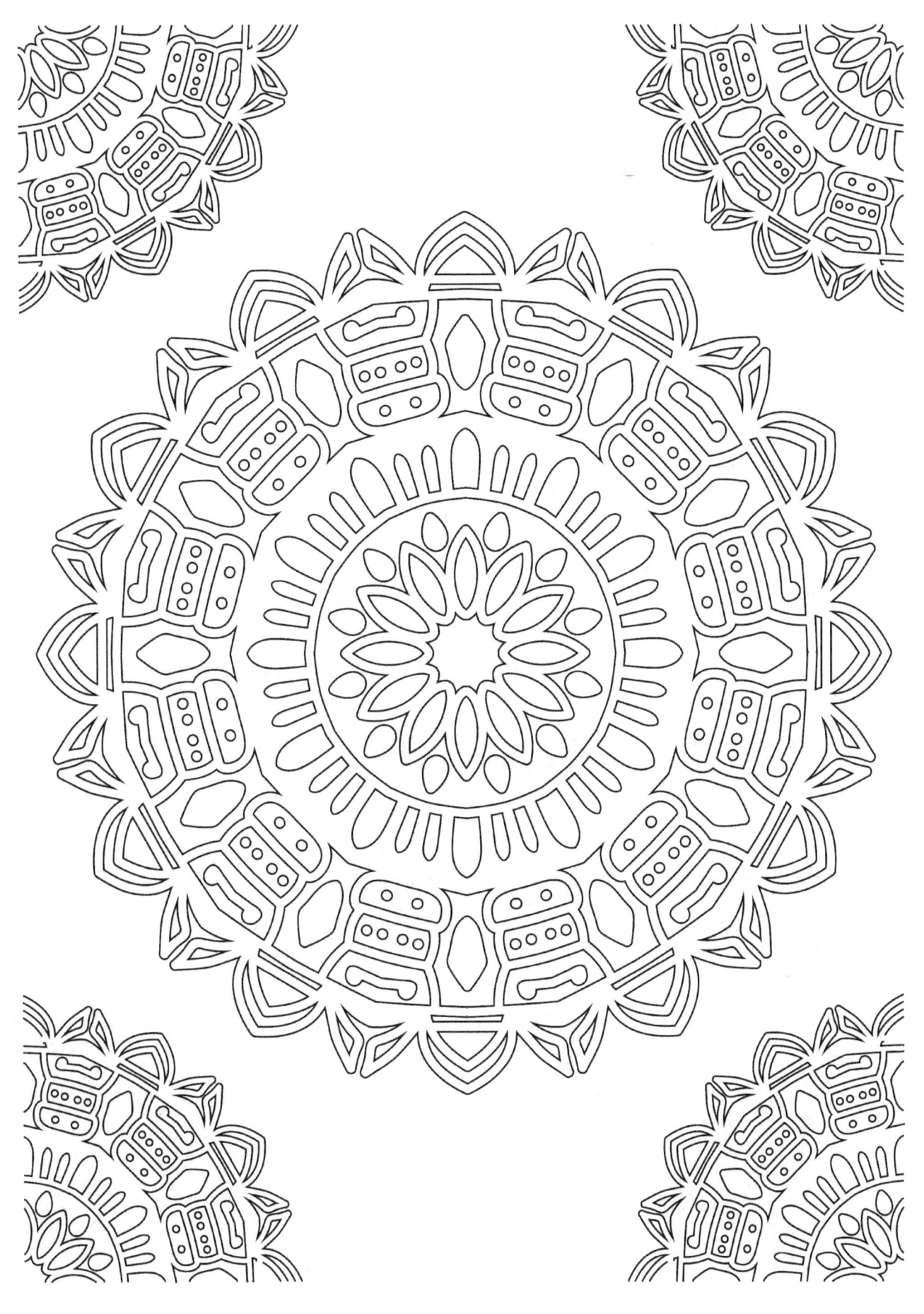

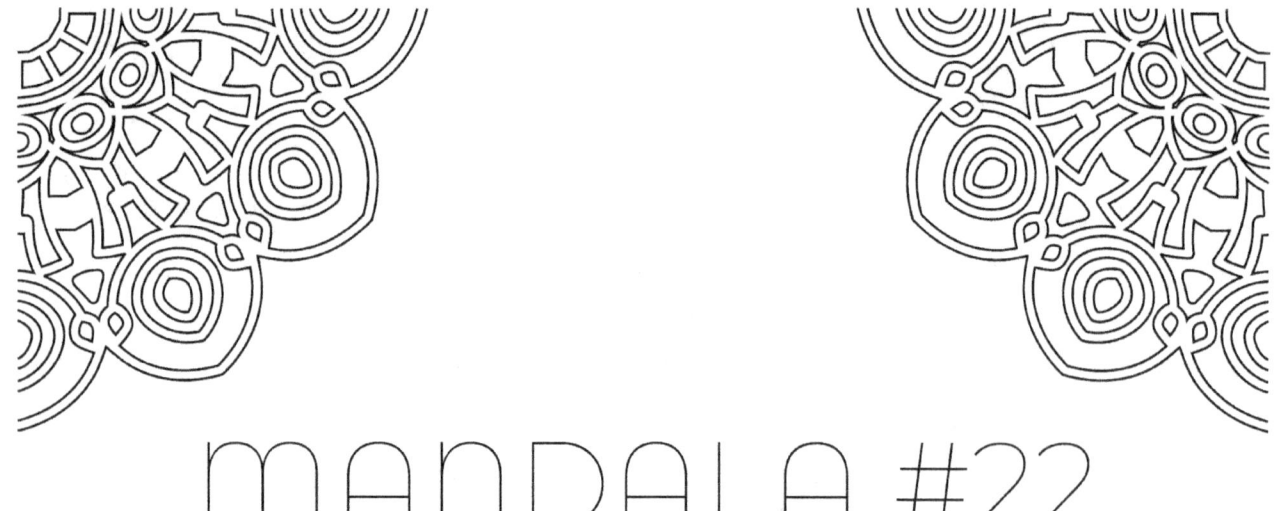

MANDALA #22

Coloring a mandala, is a great way to tune into our subconscious and see what emotional and mental state we are in.
These 3 steps will allow you to create a personal mandala:

1. Find a comfortable place to work. Sit in a quiet place where you won't be interrupted. Concentrate on the problem you want to solve the most in the moment.

2. Fill the shape with colors that reflect your current state of mind. Let your imagination run wild. There are no rules when creating a mandala.

3. Take some time to reflect on your mandala and what it means to you, and write down the result below.

_____
_____
_____
_____

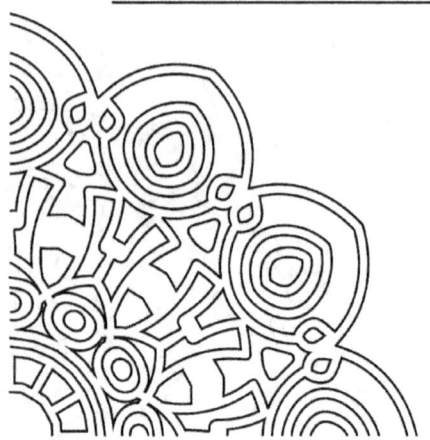
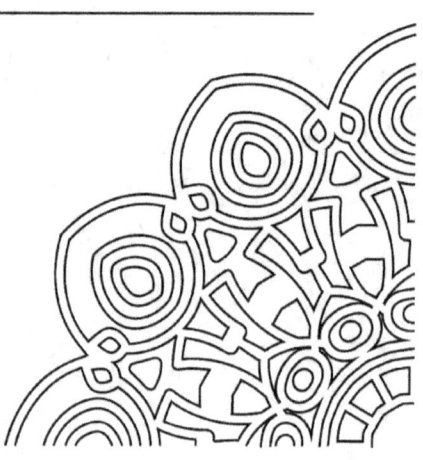

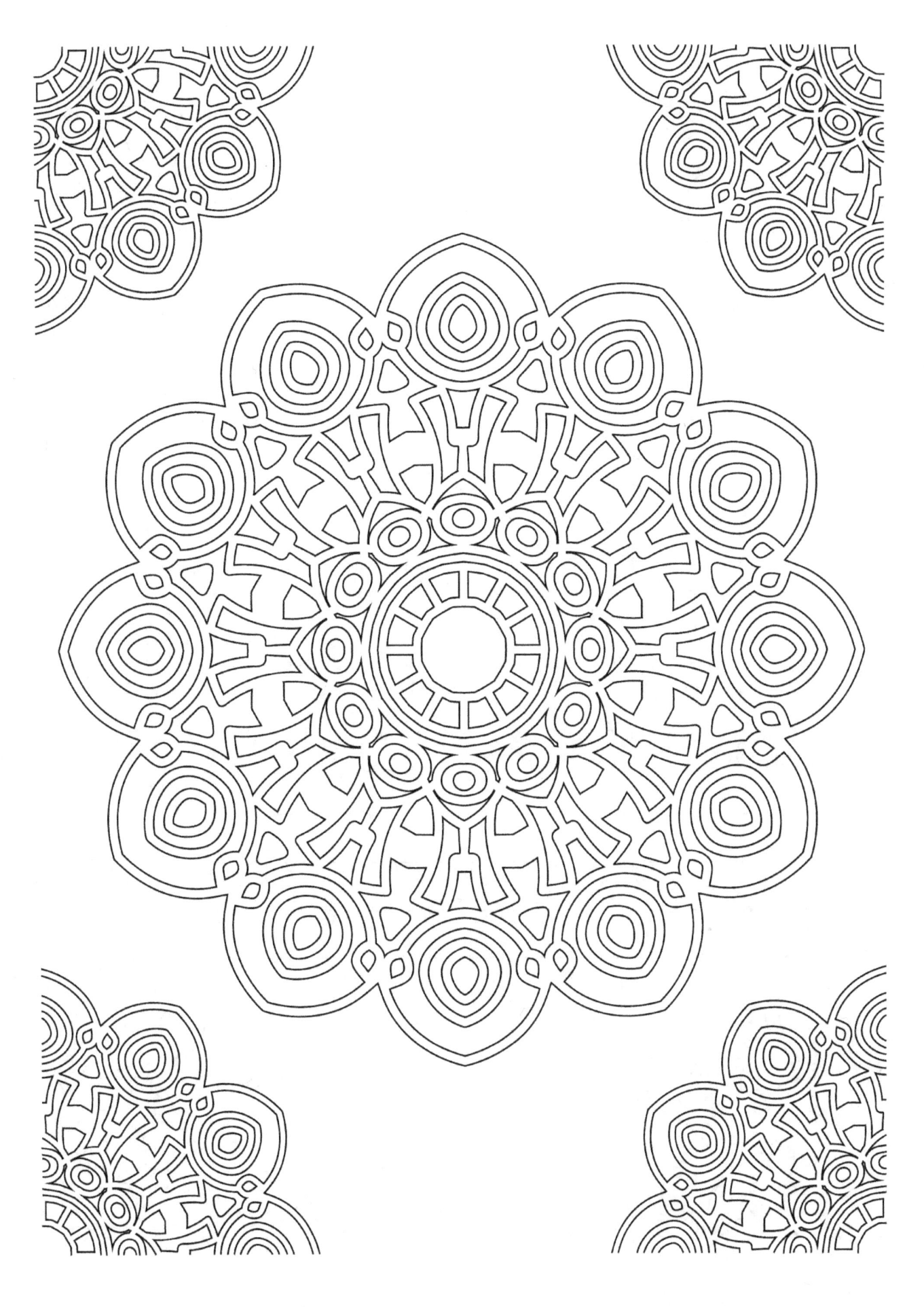

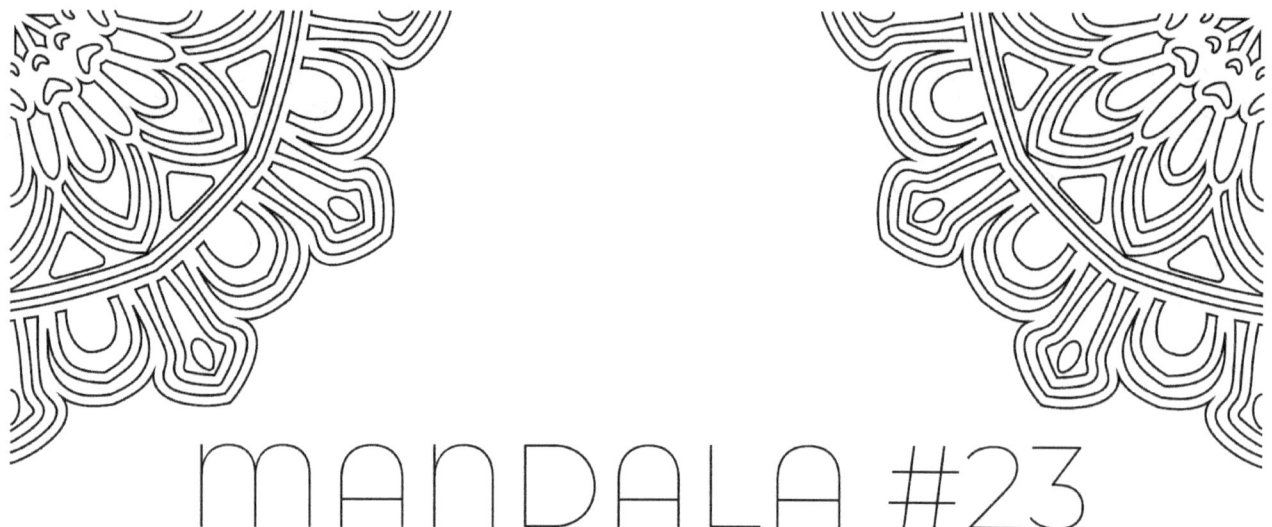

MANDALA #23

Coloring a mandala, is a great way to tune into our subconscious and see what emotional and mental state we are in.

These 3 steps will allow you to create a personal mandala:

1. Find a comfortable place to work. Sit in a quiet place where you won't be interrupted. Concentrate on the problem you want to solve the most in the moment.

2. Fill the shape with colors that reflect your current state of mind. Let your imagination run wild. There are no rules when creating a mandala.

3. Take some time to reflect on your mandala and what it means to you, and write down the result below.

_____
_____
_____
_____

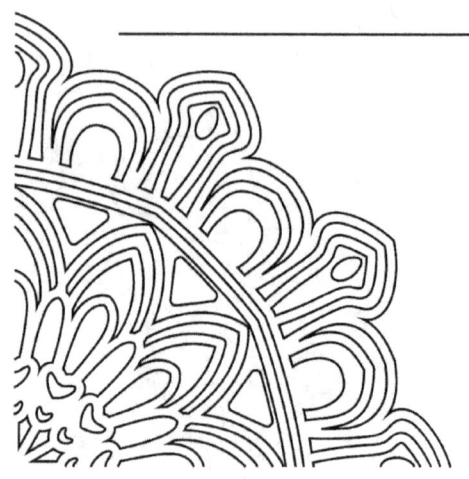
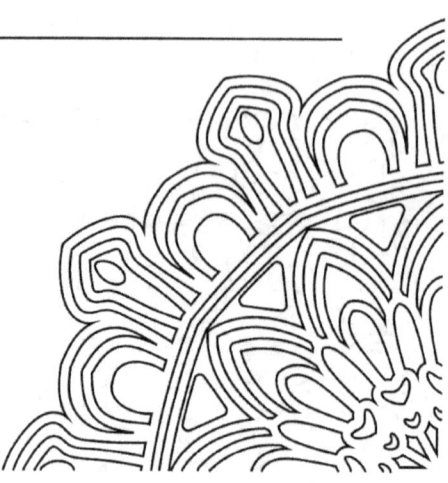

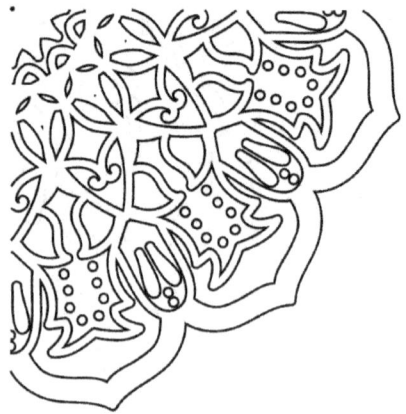
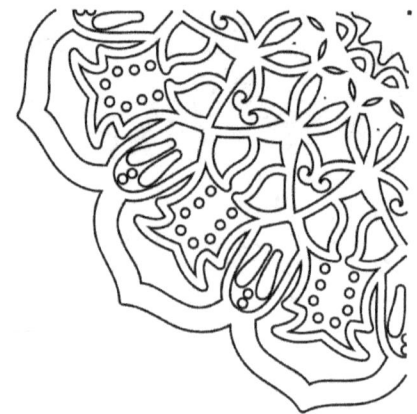

MANDALA #24

Coloring a mandala, is a great way to tune into our subconscious and see what emotional and mental state we are in.
These 3 steps will allow you to create a personal mandala:

1. Find a comfortable place to work. Sit in a quiet place where you won't be interrupted. Concentrate on the problem you want to solve the most in the moment.

2. Fill the shape with colors that reflect your current state of mind. Let your imagination run wild. There are no rules when creating a mandala.

3. Take some time to reflect on your mandala and what it means to you, and write down the result below.

_____

_____

_____

_____

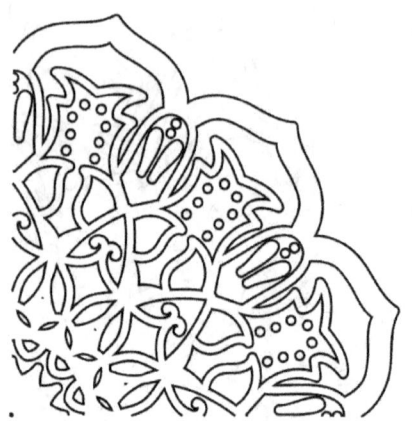
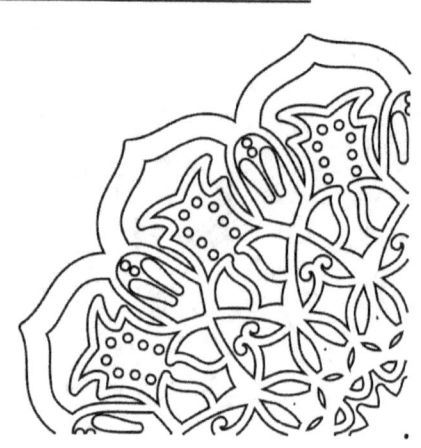

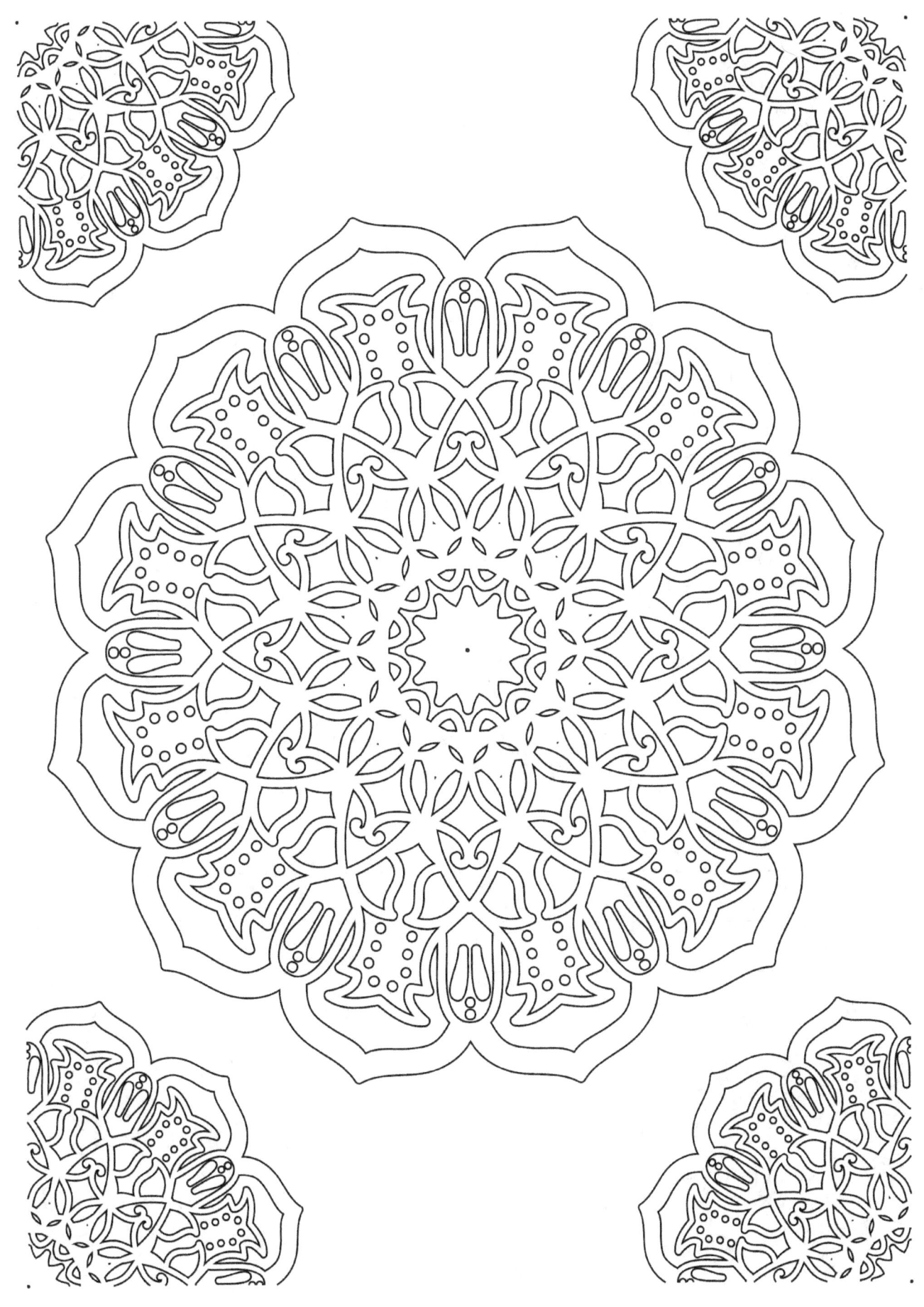

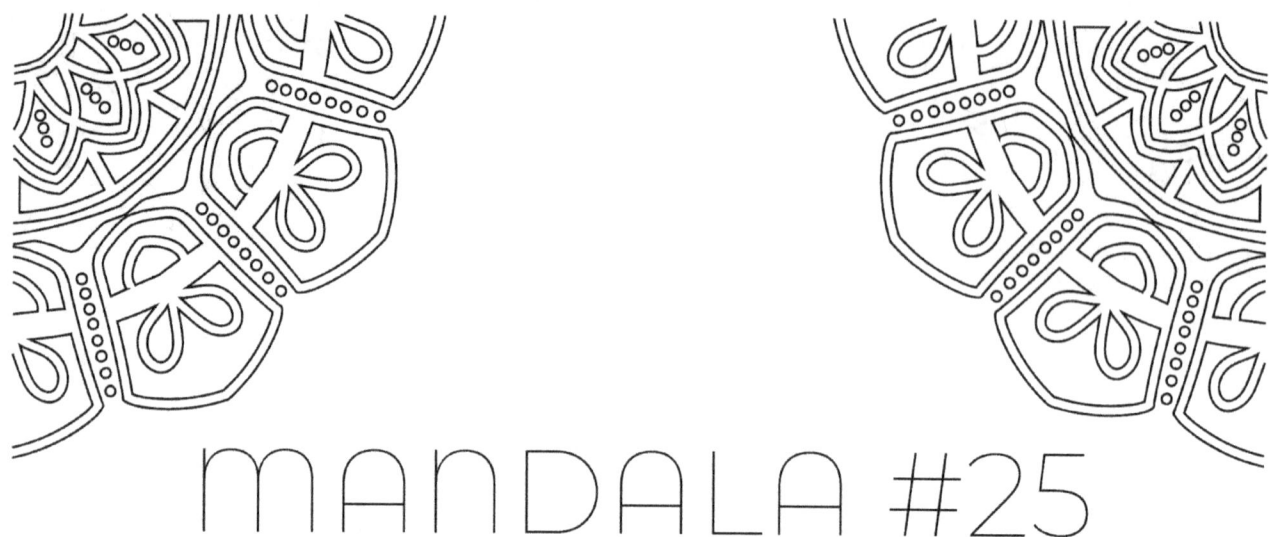

MANDALA #25

Coloring a mandala, is a great way to tune into our subconscious and see what emotional and mental state we are in.

These 3 steps will allow you to create a personal mandala:

1. Find a comfortable place to work. Sit in a quiet place where you won't be interrupted. Concentrate on the problem you want to solve the most in the moment.

2. Fill the shape with colors that reflect your current state of mind. Let your imagination run wild. There are no rules when creating a mandala.

3. Take some time to reflect on your mandala and what it means to you, and write down the result below.

_____
_____
_____
_____

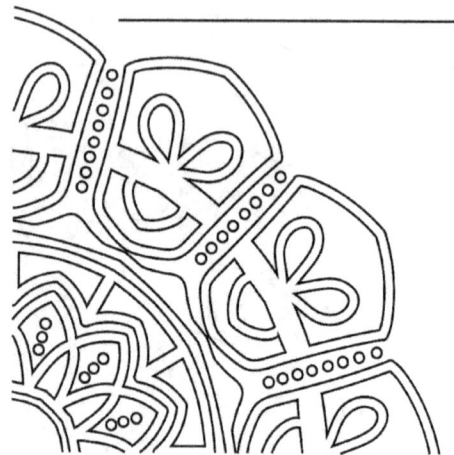
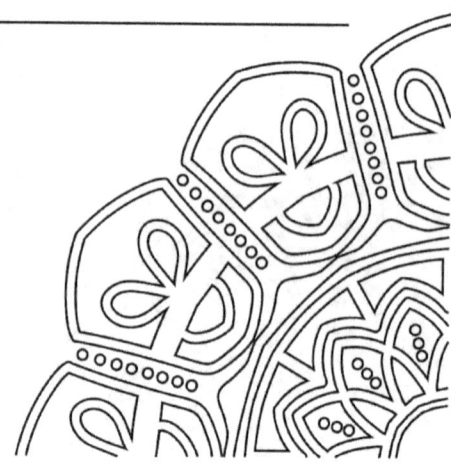

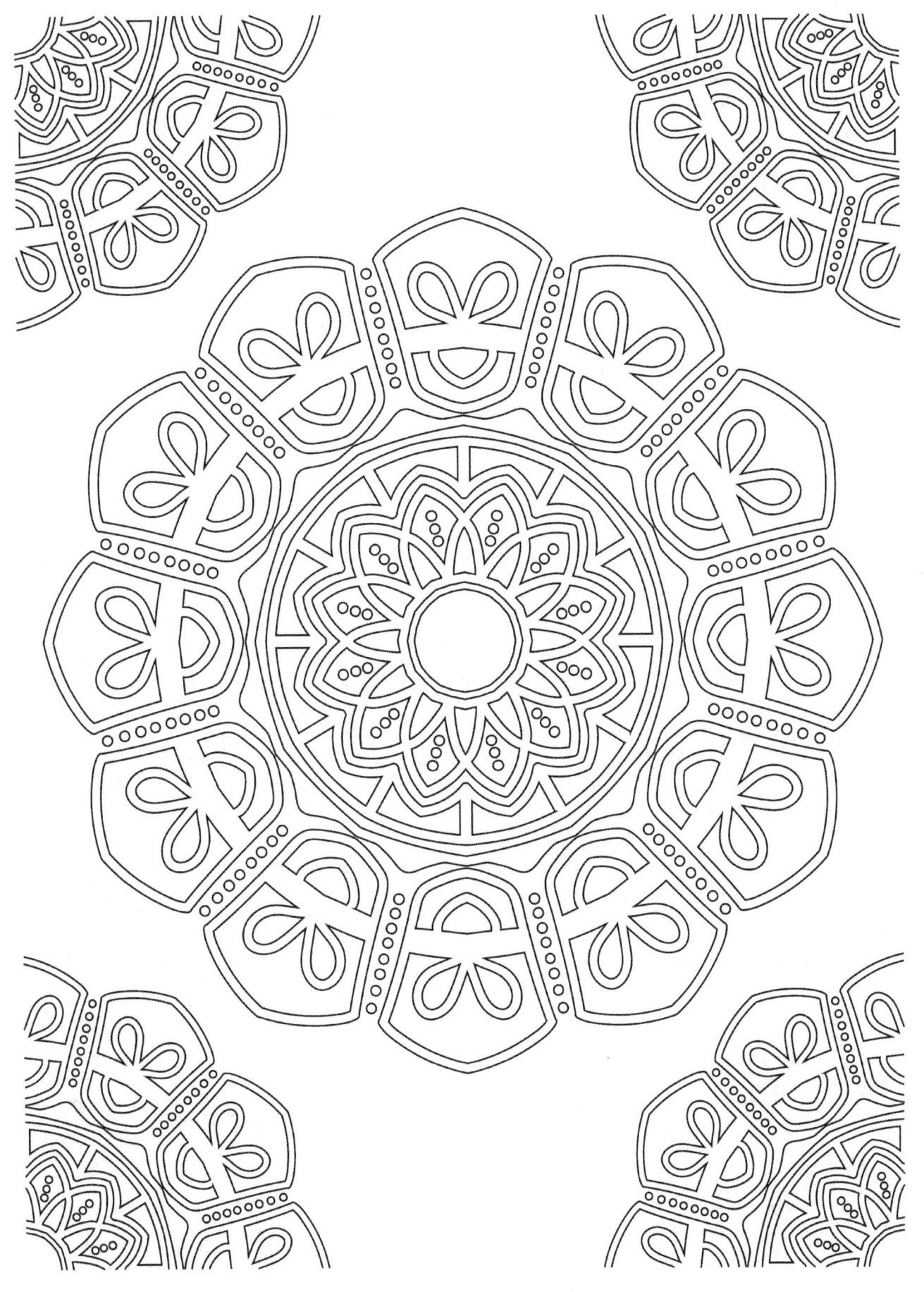

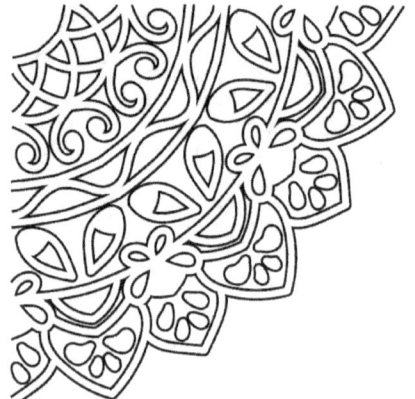
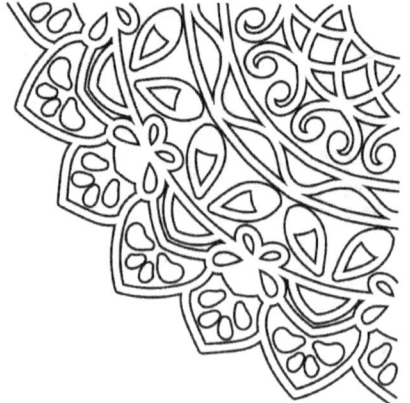

MANDALA #26

Coloring a mandala, is a great way to tune into our subconscious and see what emotional and mental state we are in.
These 3 steps will allow you to create a personal mandala:

1. Find a comfortable place to work. Sit in a quiet place where you won't be interrupted. Concentrate on the problem you want to solve the most in the moment.

2. Fill the shape with colors that reflect your current state of mind. Let your imagination run wild. There are no rules when creating a mandala.

3. Take some time to reflect on your mandala and what it means to you, and write down the result below.

_____
_____
_____
_____

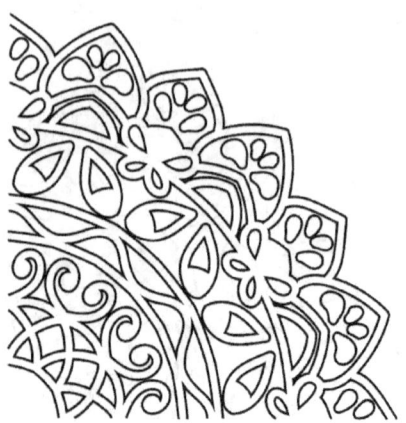
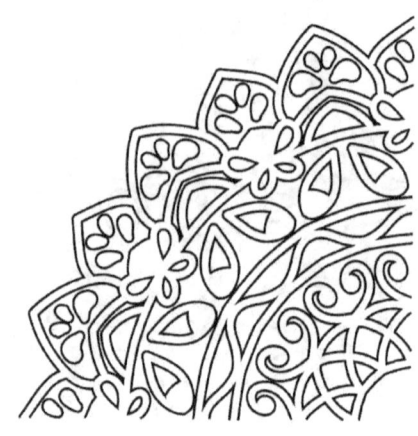

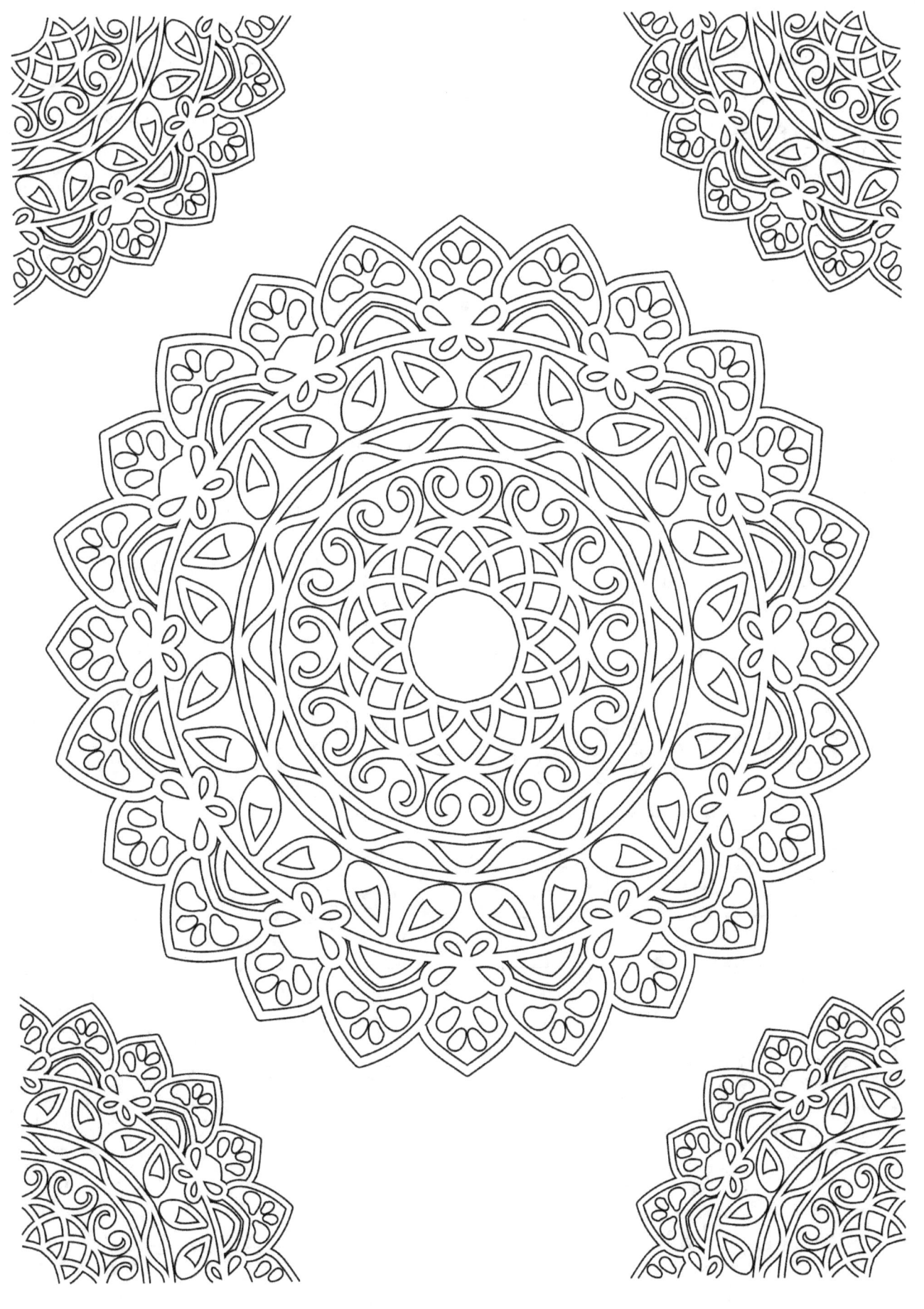

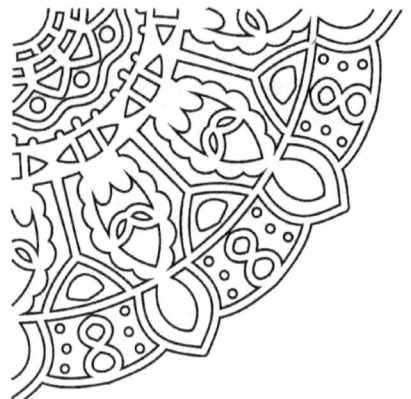
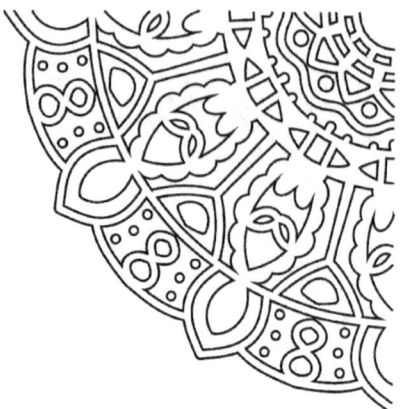

MANDALA #27

Coloring a mandala, is a great way to tune into our subconscious and see what emotional and mental state we are in.
These 3 steps will allow you to create a personal mandala:

1. Find a comfortable place to work. Sit in a quiet place where you won't be interrupted. Concentrate on the problem you want to solve the most in the moment.

2. Fill the shape with colors that reflect your current state of mind. Let your imagination run wild. There are no rules when creating a mandala.

3. Take some time to reflect on your mandala and what it means to you, and write down the result below.

_____
_____
_____
_____

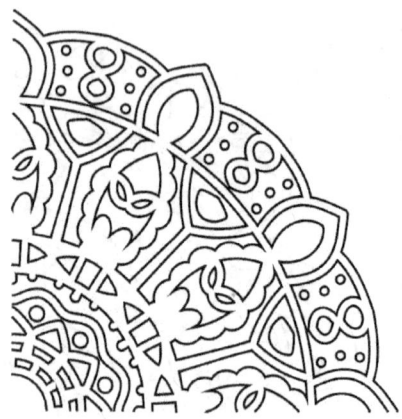
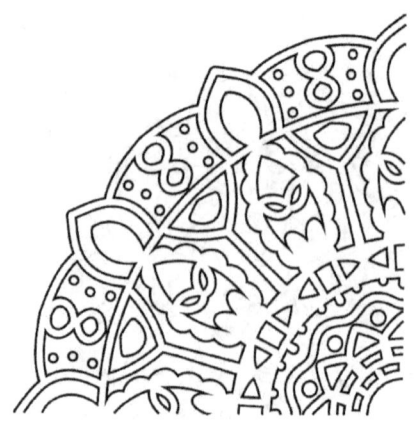

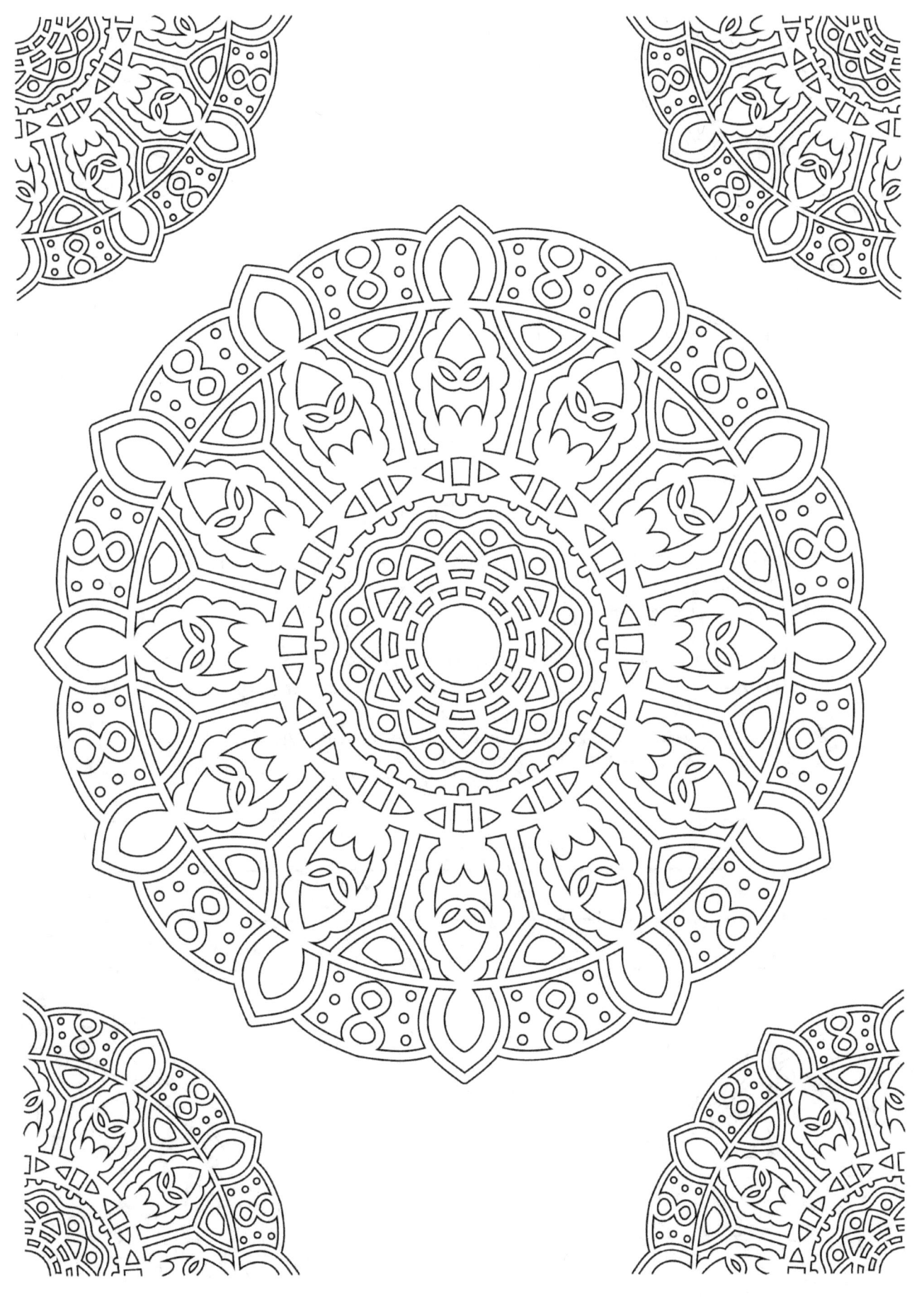

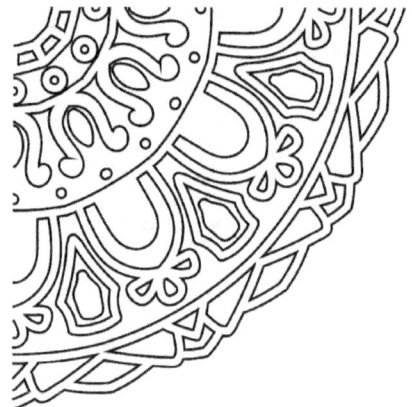
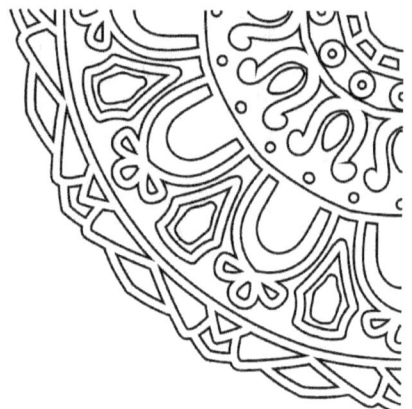

MANDALA #28

Coloring a mandala, is a great way to tune into our subconscious and see what emotional and mental state we are in.
These 3 steps will allow you to create a personal mandala:

1. Find a comfortable place to work. Sit in a quiet place where you won't be interrupted. Concentrate on the problem you want to solve the most in the moment.

2. Fill the shape with colors that reflect your current state of mind. Let your imagination run wild. There are no rules when creating a mandala.

3. Take some time to reflect on your mandala and what it means to you, and write down the result below.

_____

_____

_____

_____

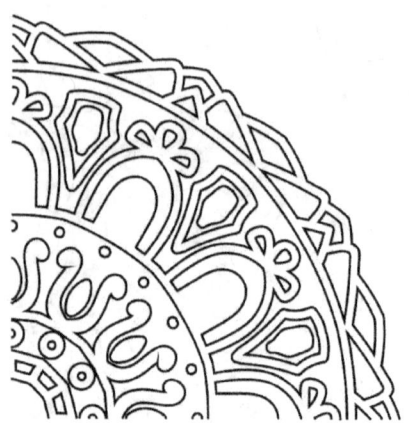
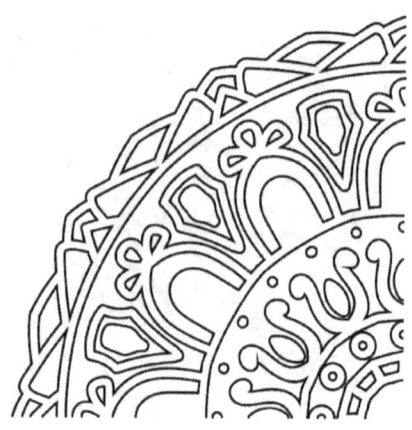

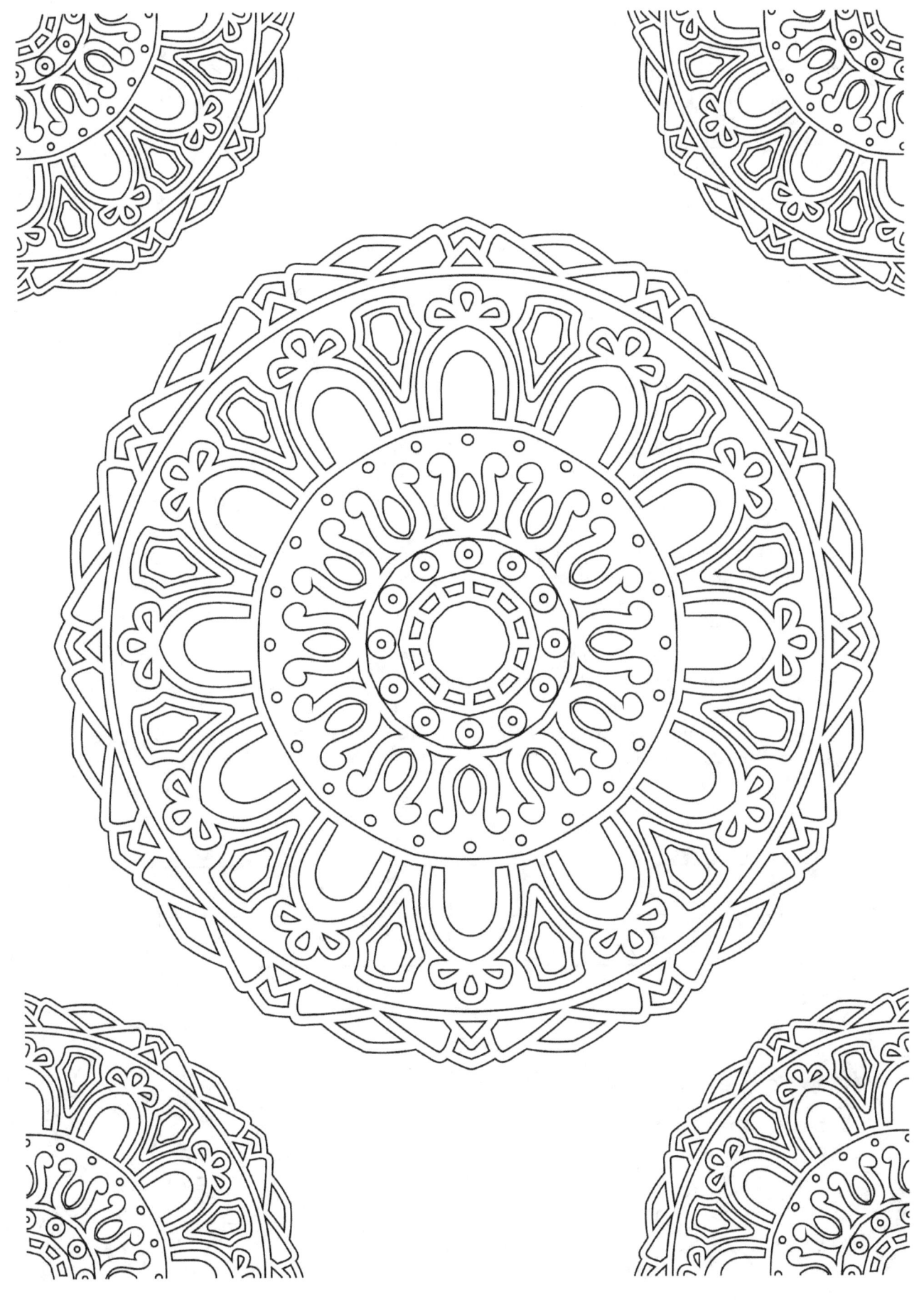

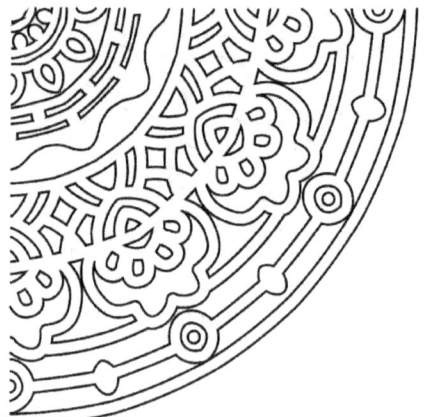 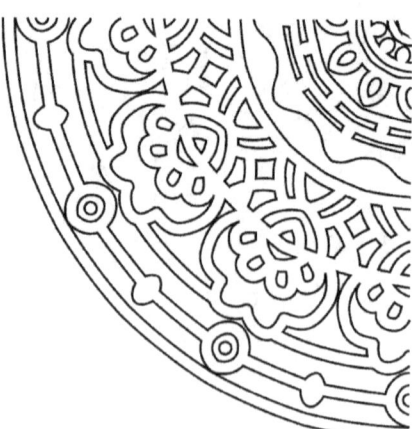

MANDALA #29

Coloring a mandala, is a great way to tune into our subconscious and see what emotional and mental state we are in.

These 3 steps will allow you to create a personal mandala:

1. Find a comfortable place to work. Sit in a quiet place where you won't be interrupted. Concentrate on the problem you want to solve the most in the moment.

2. Fill the shape with colors that reflect your current state of mind. Let your imagination run wild. There are no rules when creating a mandala.

3. Take some time to reflect on your mandala and what it means to you, and write down the result below.

_____

_____

_____

_____

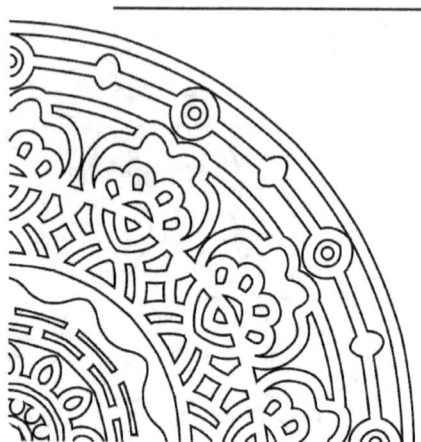 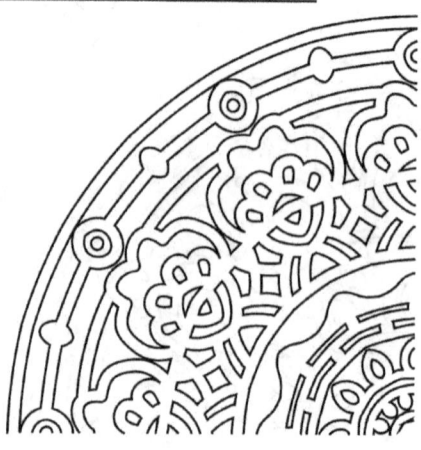

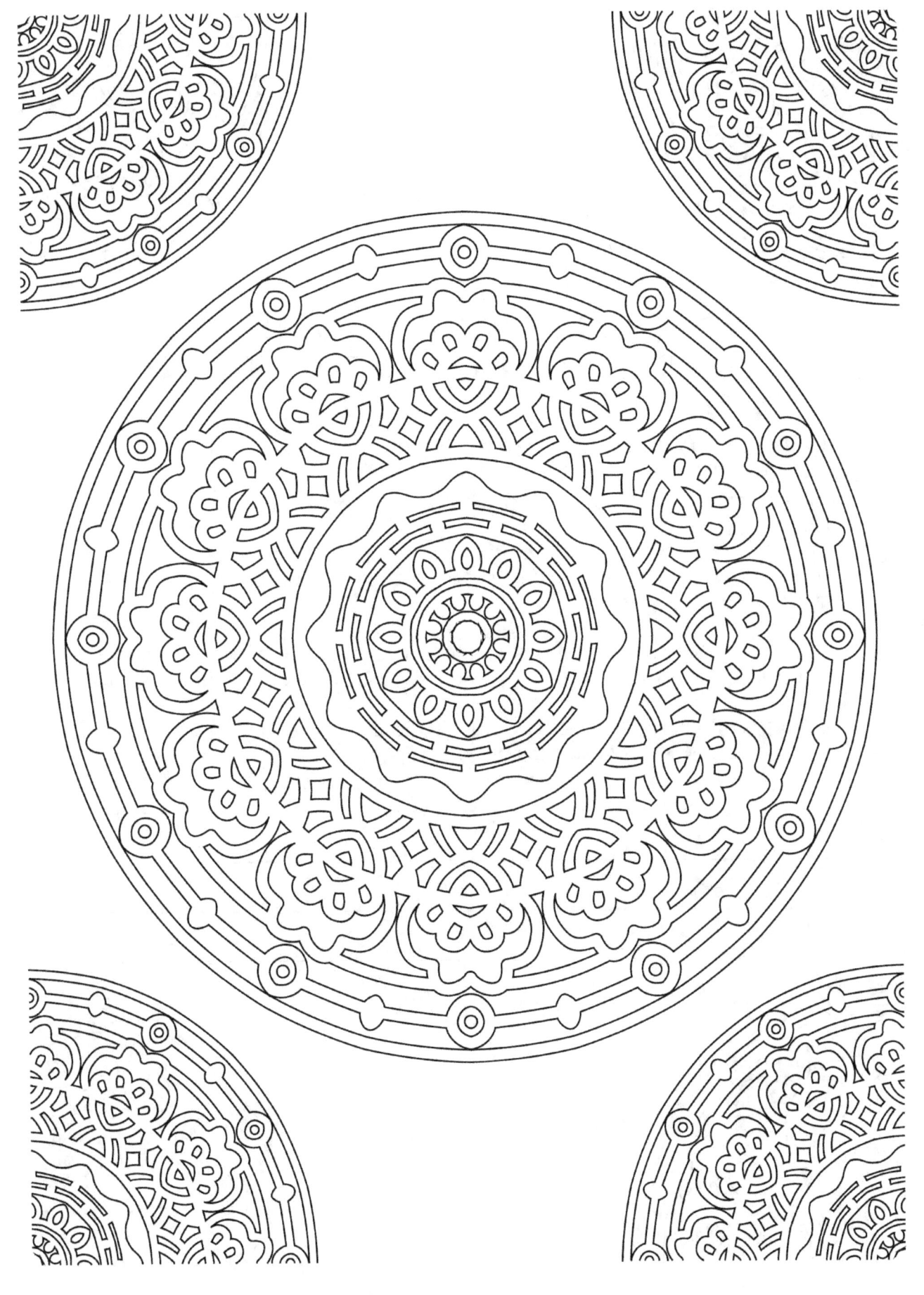

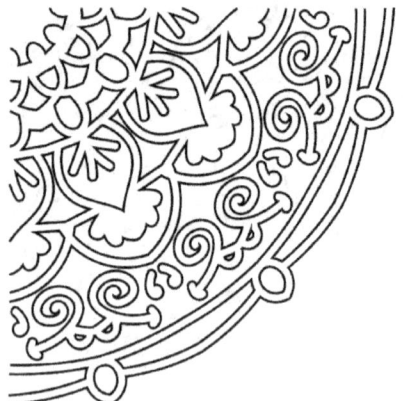
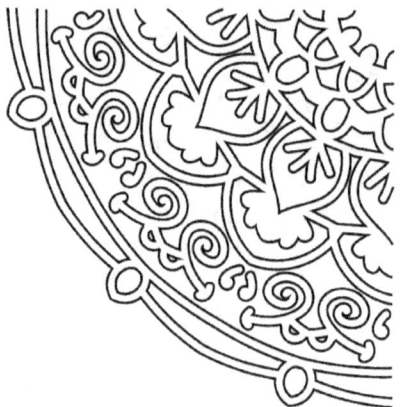

MANDALA #30

Coloring a mandala, is a great way to tune into our subconscious and see what emotional and mental state we are in.
These 3 steps will allow you to create a personal mandala:

1. Find a comfortable place to work. Sit in a quiet place where you won't be interrupted. Concentrate on the problem you want to solve the most in the moment.

2. Fill the shape with colors that reflect your current state of mind. Let your imagination run wild. There are no rules when creating a mandala.

3. Take some time to reflect on your mandala and what it means to you, and write down the result below.

_____

_____

_____

_____

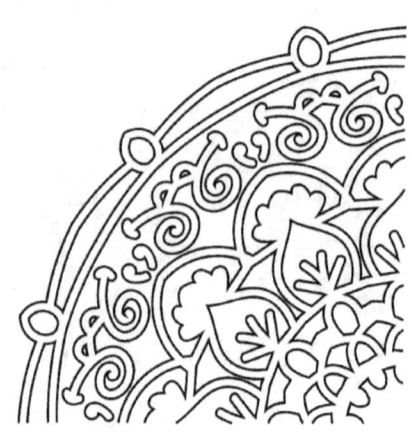

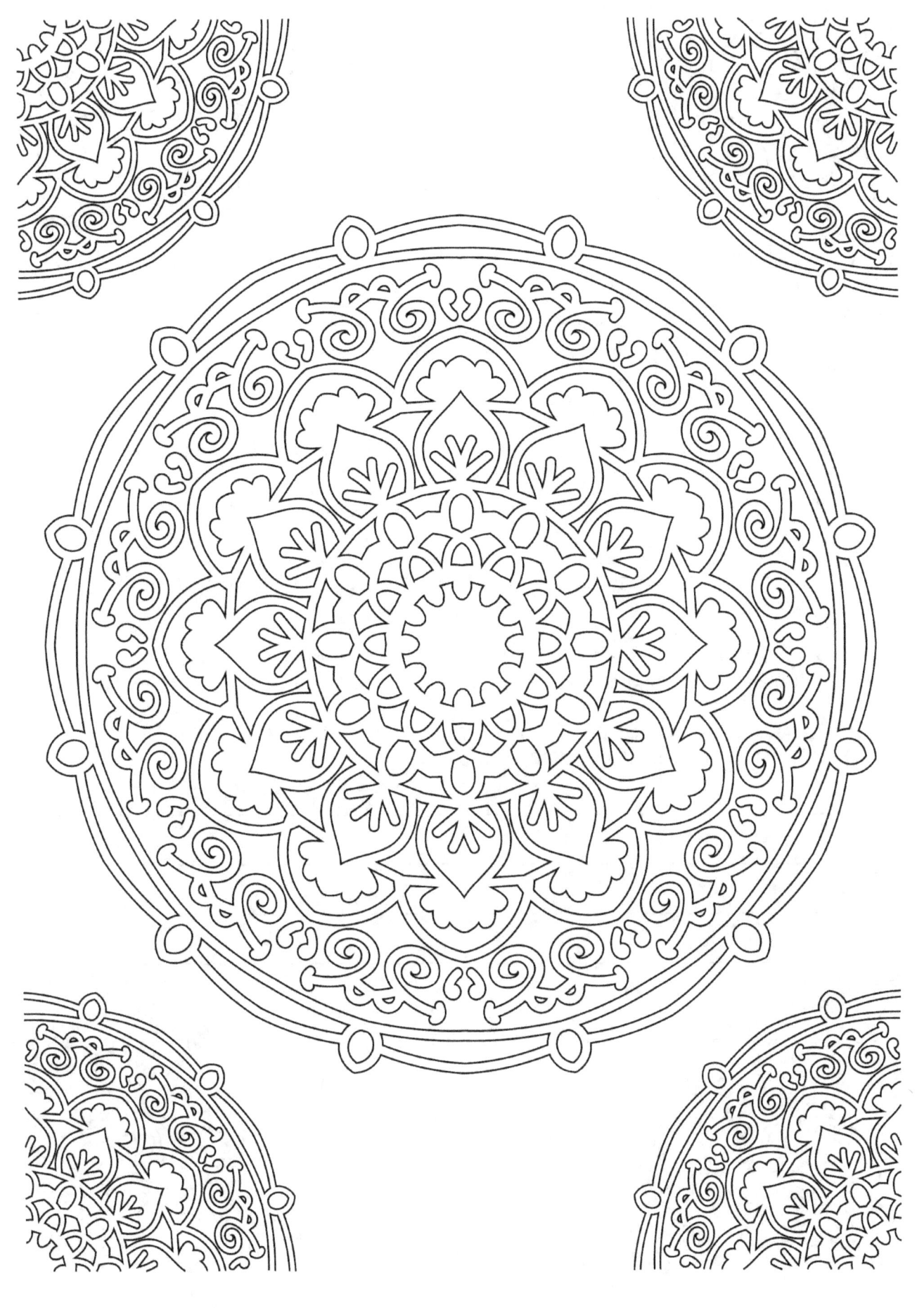

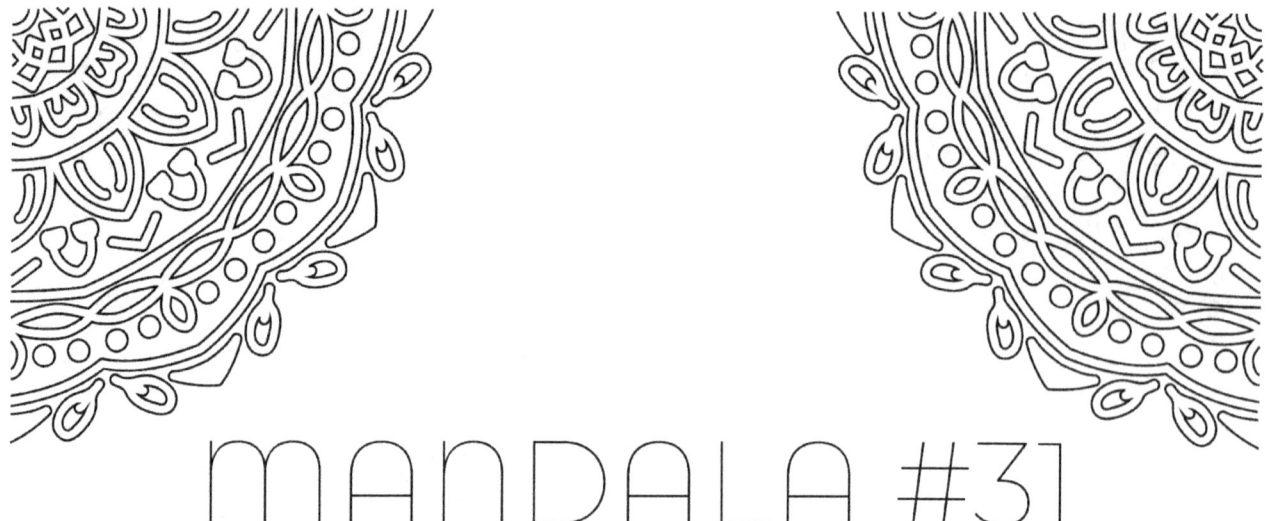

MANDALA #31

Coloring a mandala, is a great way to tune into our subconscious and see what emotional and mental state we are in.
These 3 steps will allow you to create a personal mandala:

1. Find a comfortable place to work. Sit in a quiet place where you won't be interrupted. Concentrate on the problem you want to solve the most in the moment.

2. Fill the shape with colors that reflect your current state of mind. Let your imagination run wild. There are no rules when creating a mandala.

3. Take some time to reflect on your mandala and what it means to you, and write down the result below.

_____
_____
_____
_____

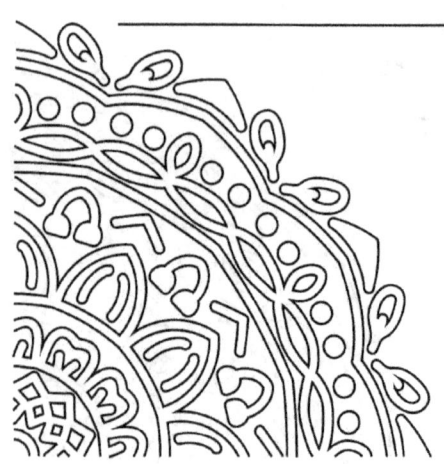
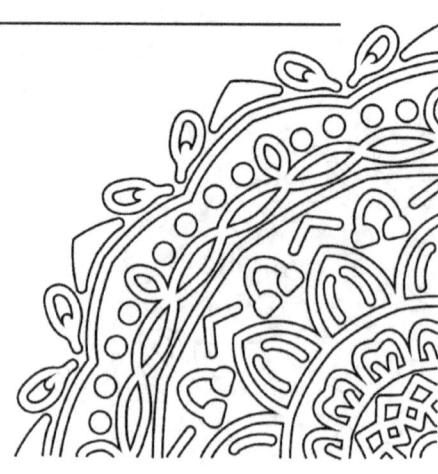

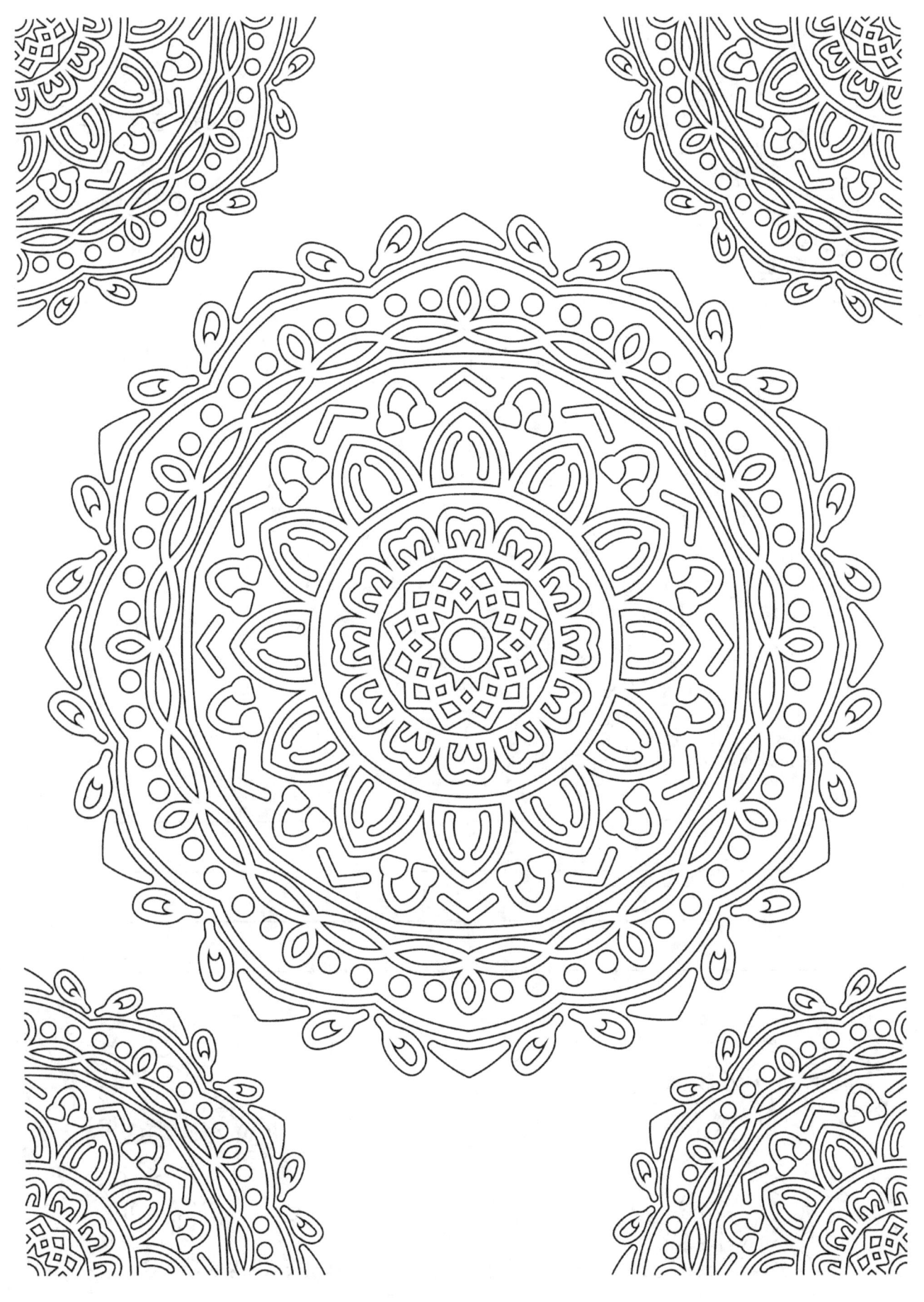

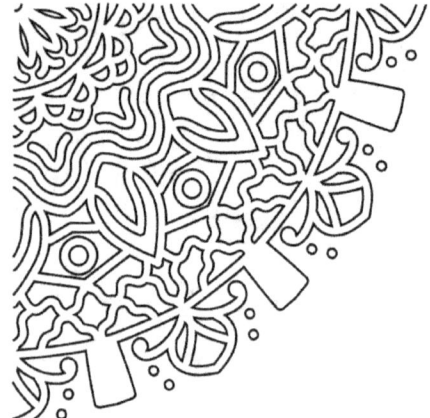
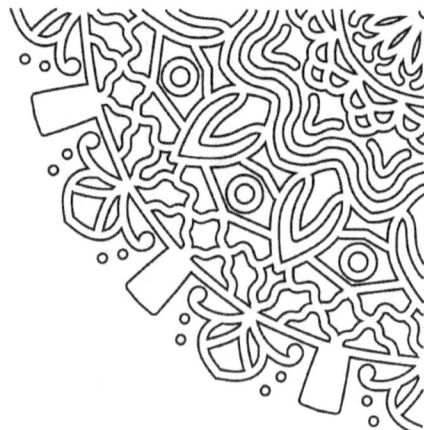

MANDALA #32

Coloring a mandala, is a great way to tune into our subconscious and see what emotional and mental state we are in.
These 3 steps will allow you to create a personal mandala:

1. Find a comfortable place to work. Sit in a quiet place where you won't be interrupted. Concentrate on the problem you want to solve the most in the moment.

2. Fill the shape with colors that reflect your current state of mind. Let your imagination run wild. There are no rules when creating a mandala.

3. Take some time to reflect on your mandala and what it means to you, and write down the result below.

_____
_____
_____
_____

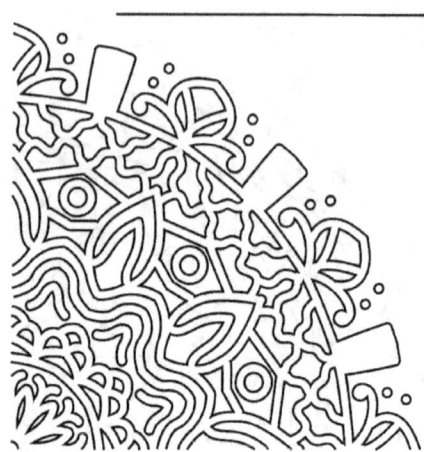
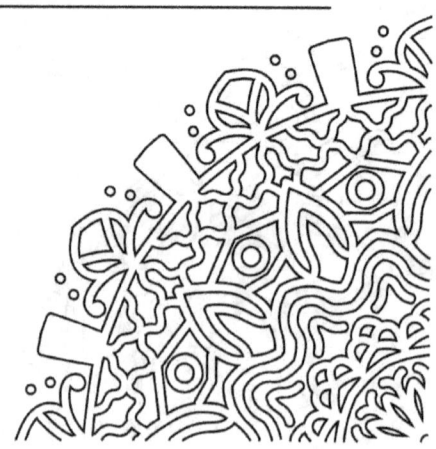

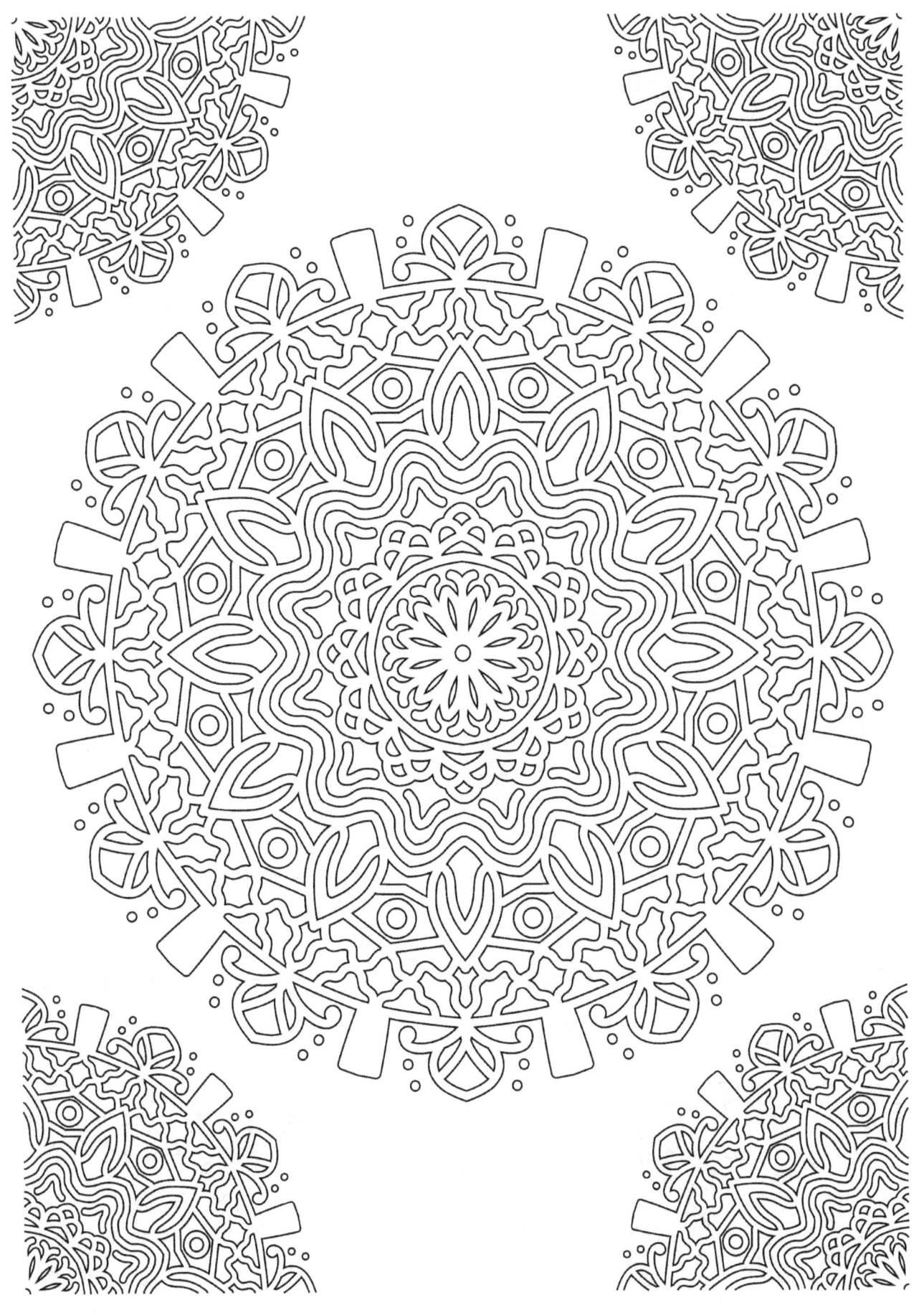

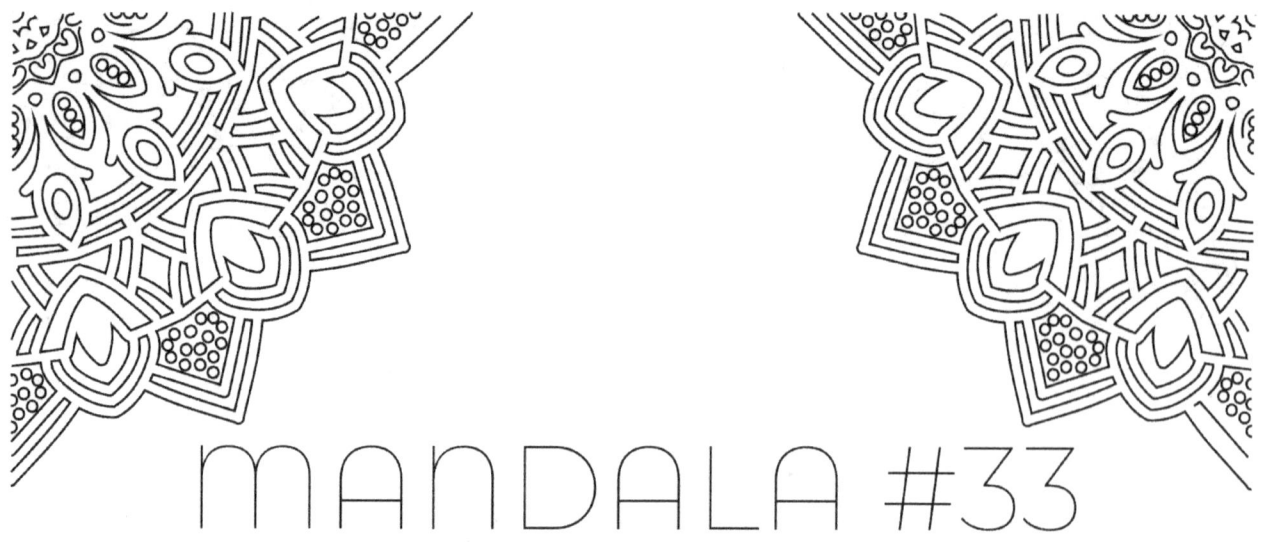

MANDALA #33

Coloring a mandala, is a great way to tune into our subconscious and see what emotional and mental state we are in.

These 3 steps will allow you to create a personal mandala:

1. Find a comfortable place to work. Sit in a quiet place where you won't be interrupted. Concentrate on the problem you want to solve the most in the moment.

2. Fill the shape with colors that reflect your current state of mind. Let your imagination run wild. There are no rules when creating a mandala.

3. Take some time to reflect on your mandala and what it means to you, and write down the result below.

_____

_____

_____

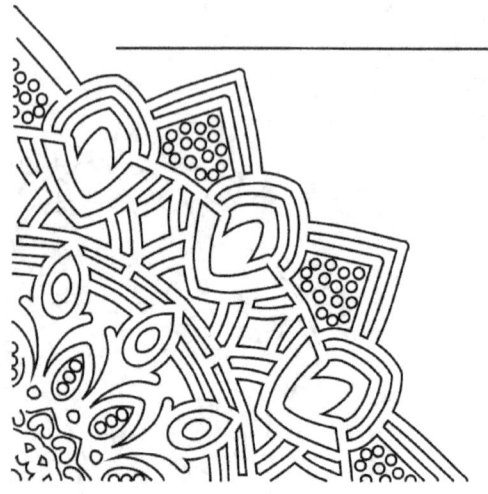
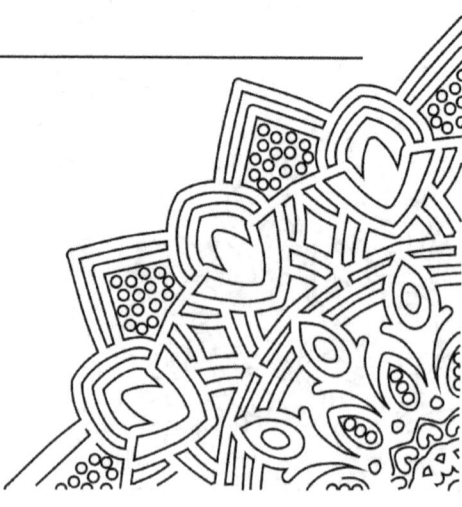

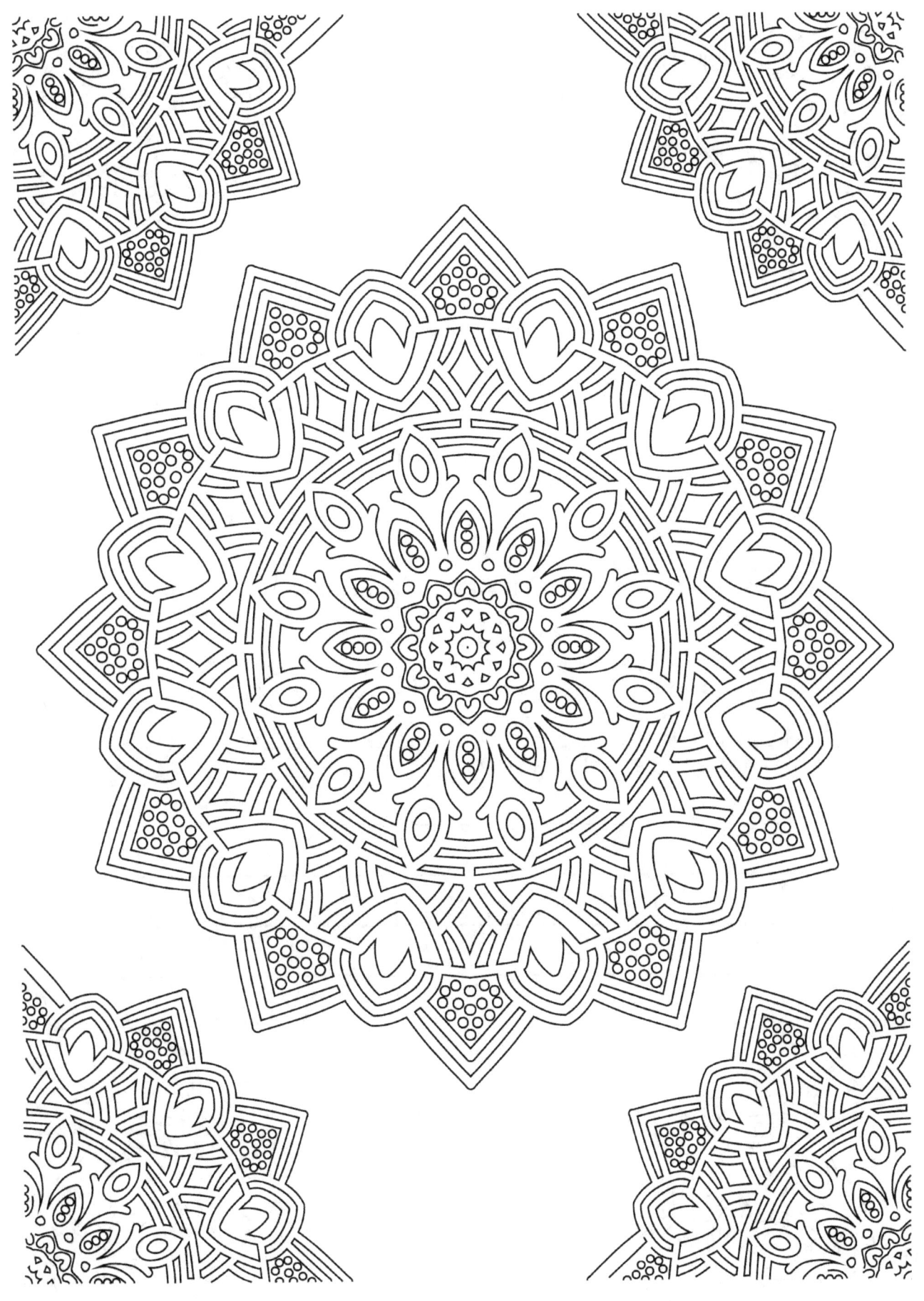

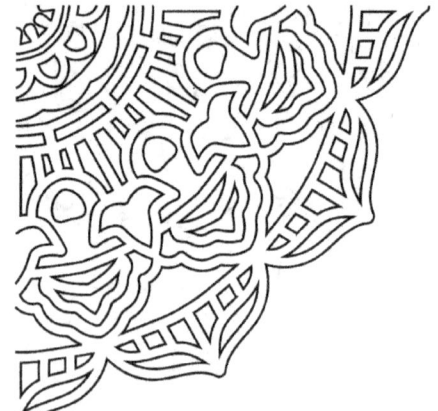
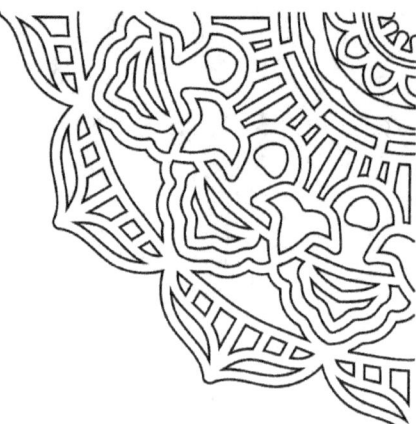

MANDALA #34

Coloring a mandala, is a great way to tune into our subconscious and see what emotional and mental state we are in.
These 3 steps will allow you to create a personal mandala:

1. Find a comfortable place to work. Sit in a quiet place where you won't be interrupted. Concentrate on the problem you want to solve the most in the moment.

2. Fill the shape with colors that reflect your current state of mind. Let your imagination run wild. There are no rules when creating a mandala.

3. Take some time to reflect on your mandala and what it means to you, and write down the result below.

_____
_____
_____
_____

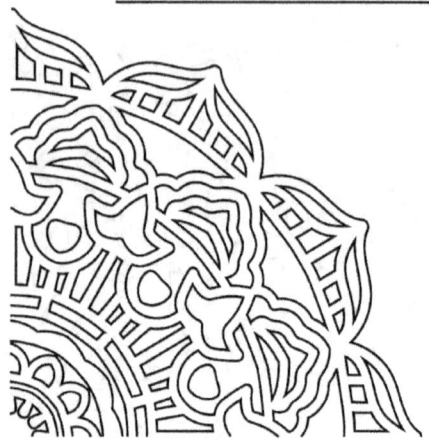
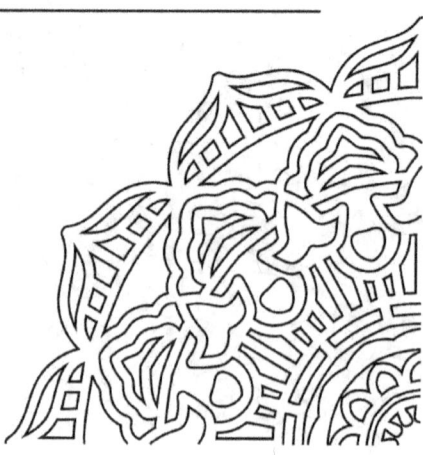

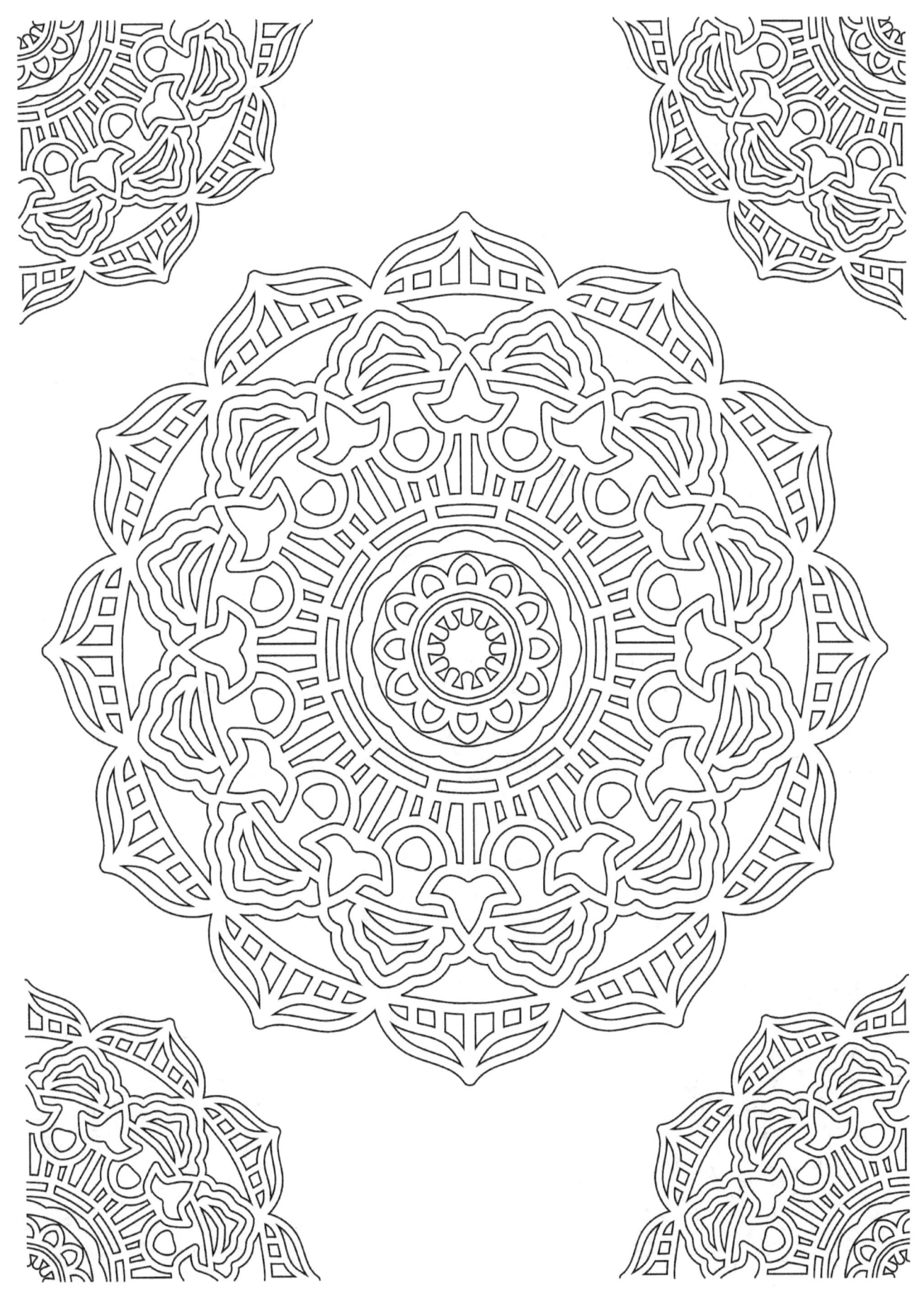

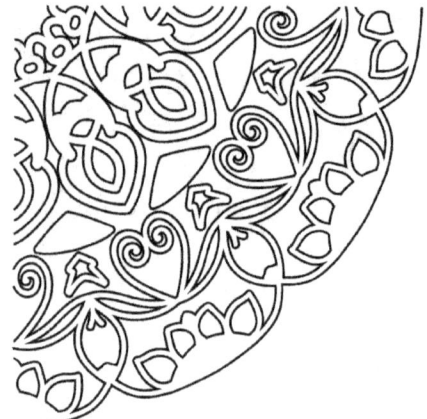
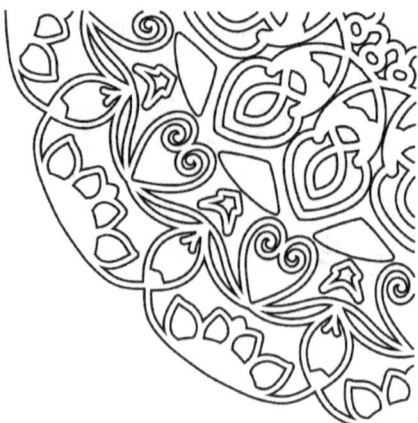

MANDALA #35

Coloring a mandala, is a great way to tune into our subconscious and see what emotional and mental state we are in.

These 3 steps will allow you to create a personal mandala:

1. Find a comfortable place to work. Sit in a quiet place where you won't be interrupted. Concentrate on the problem you want to solve the most in the moment.

2. Fill the shape with colors that reflect your current state of mind. Let your imagination run wild. There are no rules when creating a mandala.

3. Take some time to reflect on your mandala and what it means to you, and write down the result below.

_____
_____
_____
_____

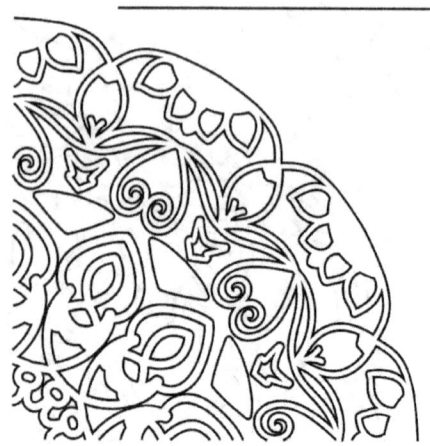
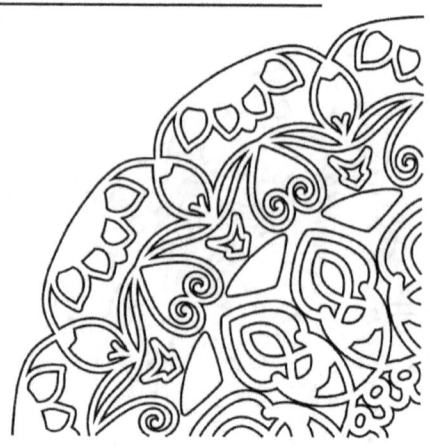

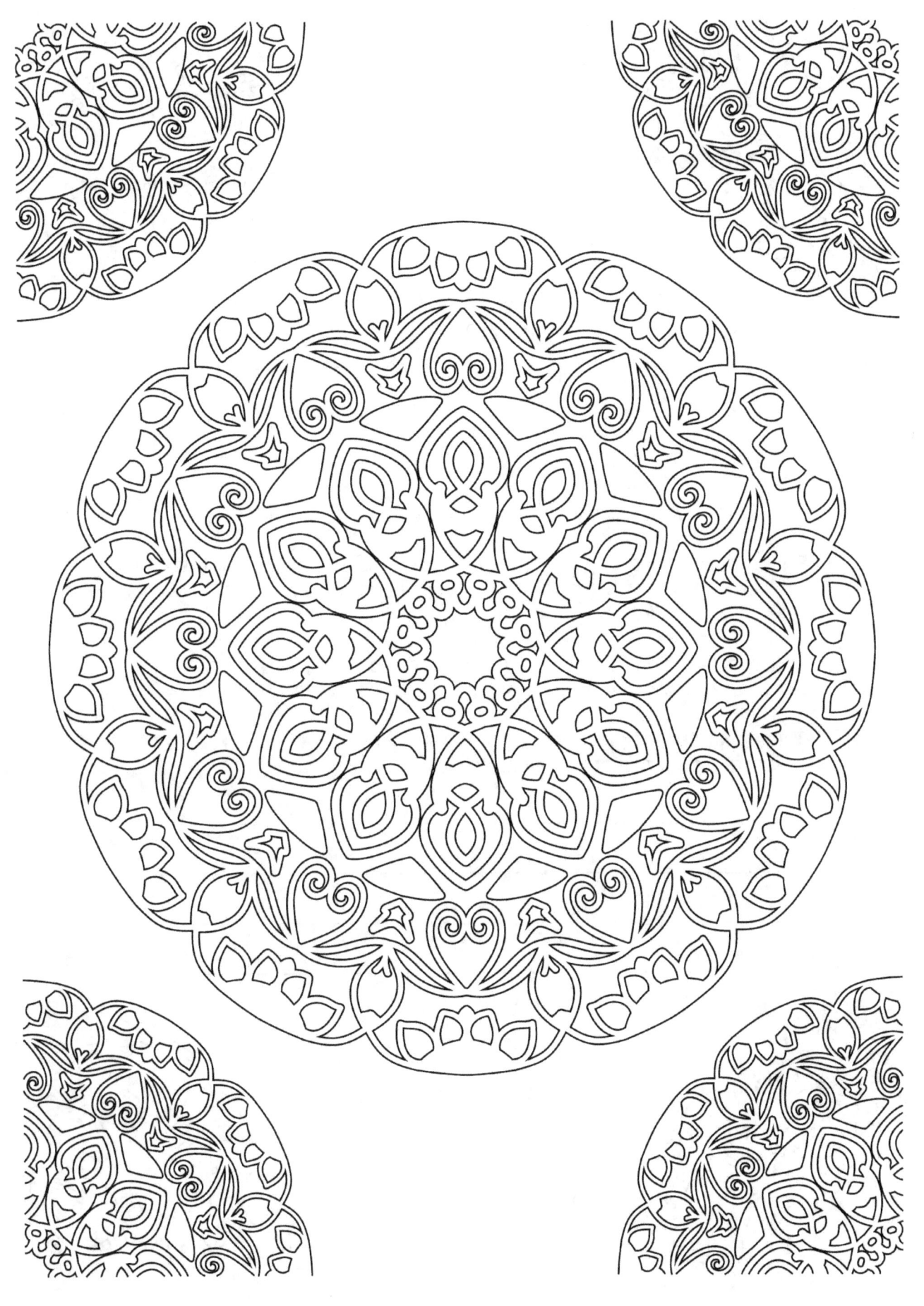

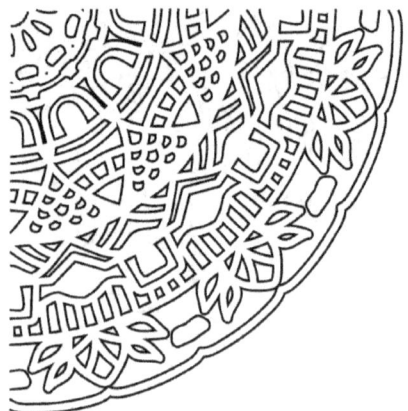
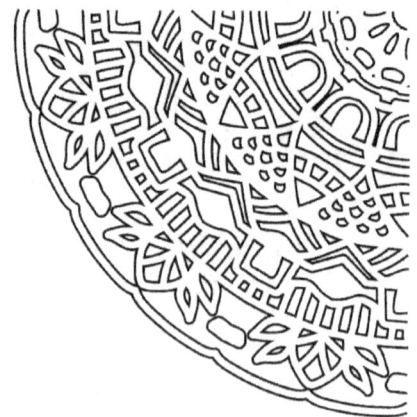

MANDALA #36

Coloring a mandala, is a great way to tune into our subconscious and see what emotional and mental state we are in.
These 3 steps will allow you to create a personal mandala:

1. Find a comfortable place to work. Sit in a quiet place where you won't be interrupted. Concentrate on the problem you want to solve the most in the moment.

2. Fill the shape with colors that reflect your current state of mind. Let your imagination run wild. There are no rules when creating a mandala.

3. Take some time to reflect on your mandala and what it means to you, and write down the result below.

_____
_____
_____
_____

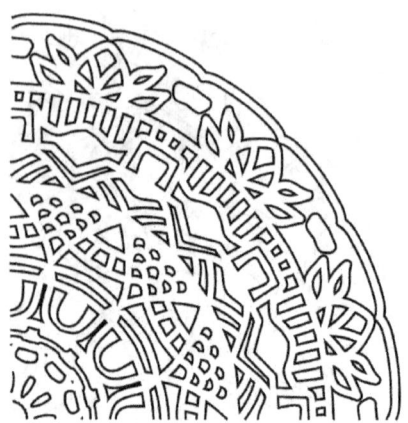
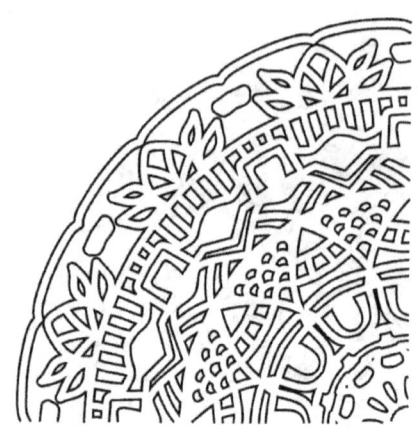

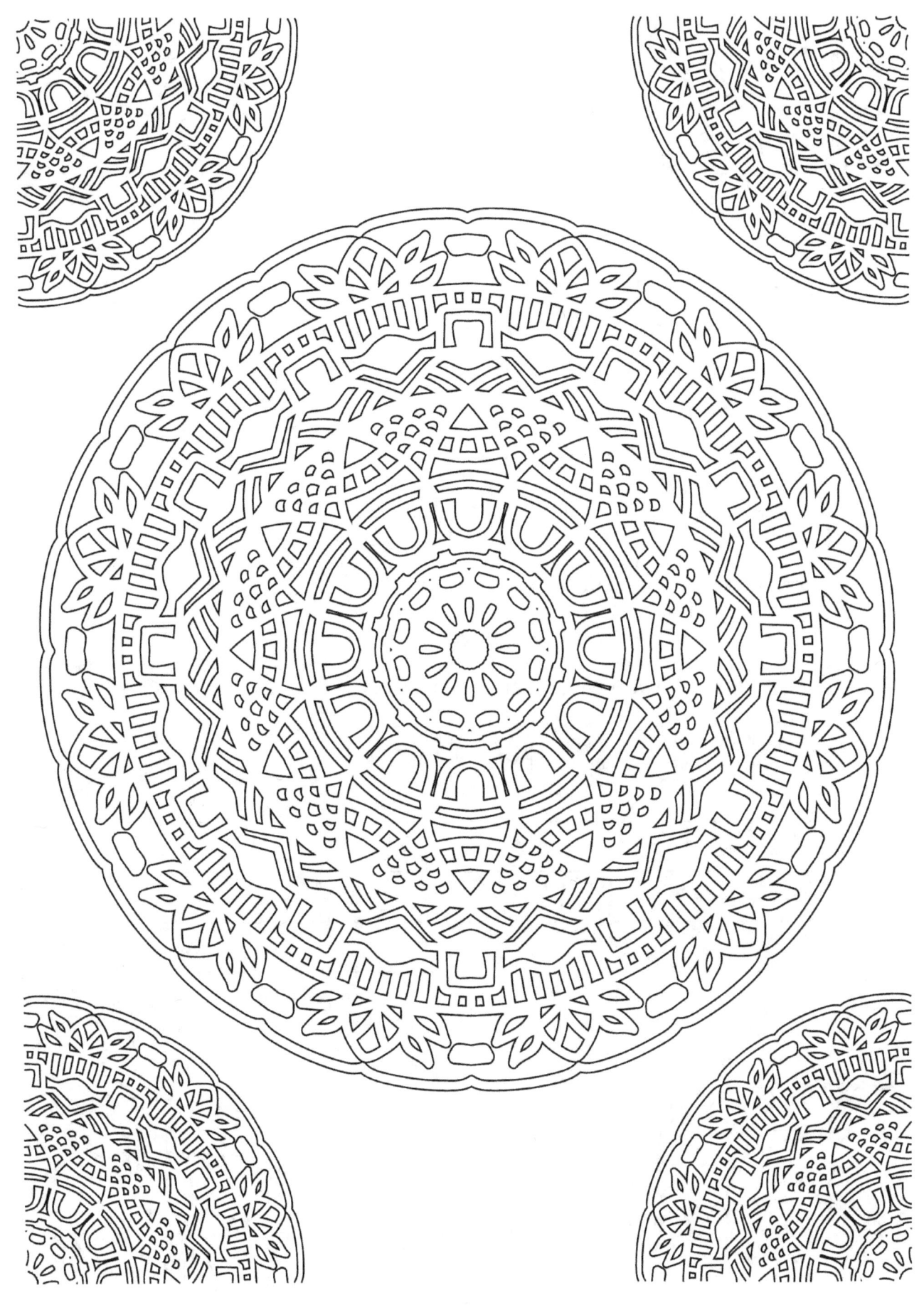

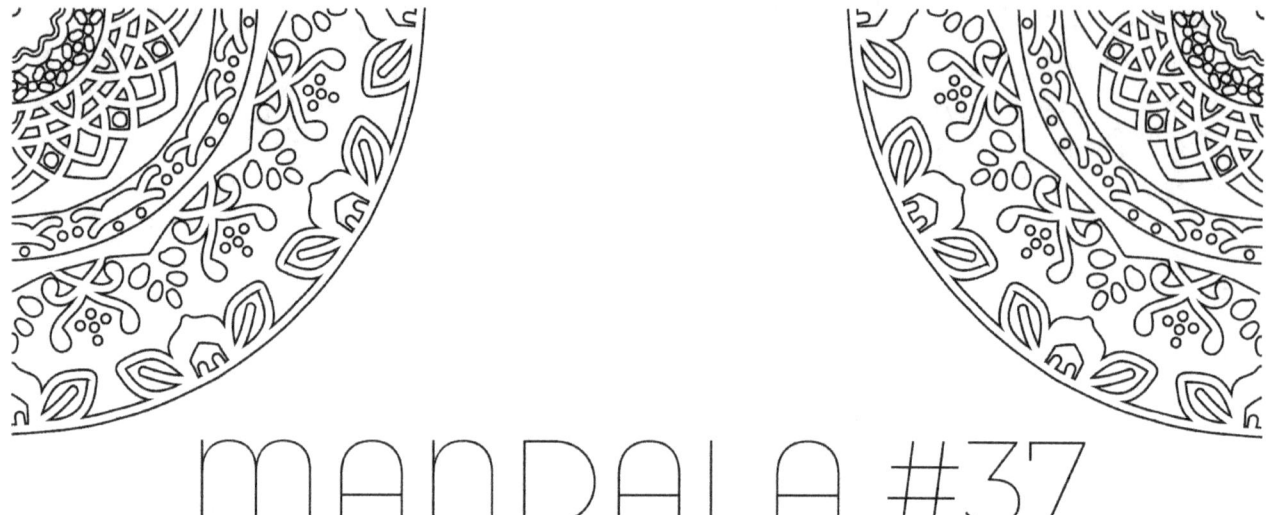

MANDALA #37

Coloring a mandala, is a great way to tune into our subconscious and see what emotional and mental state we are in.

These 3 steps will allow you to create a personal mandala:

1. Find a comfortable place to work. Sit in a quiet place where you won't be interrupted. Concentrate on the problem you want to solve the most in the moment.

2. Fill the shape with colors that reflect your current state of mind. Let your imagination run wild. There are no rules when creating a mandala.

3. Take some time to reflect on your mandala and what it means to you, and write down the result below.

_____

_____

_____

_____

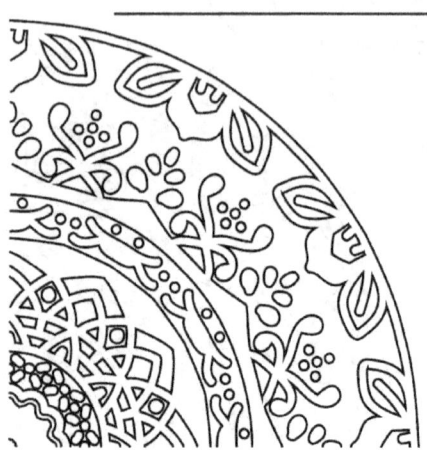
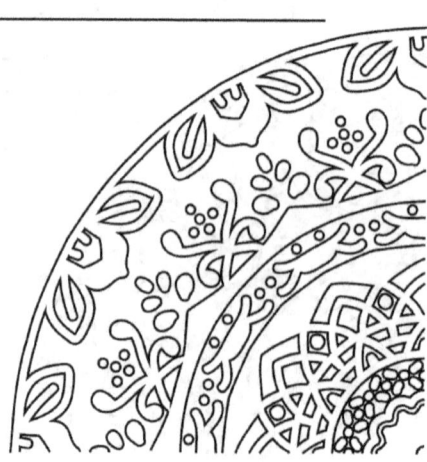

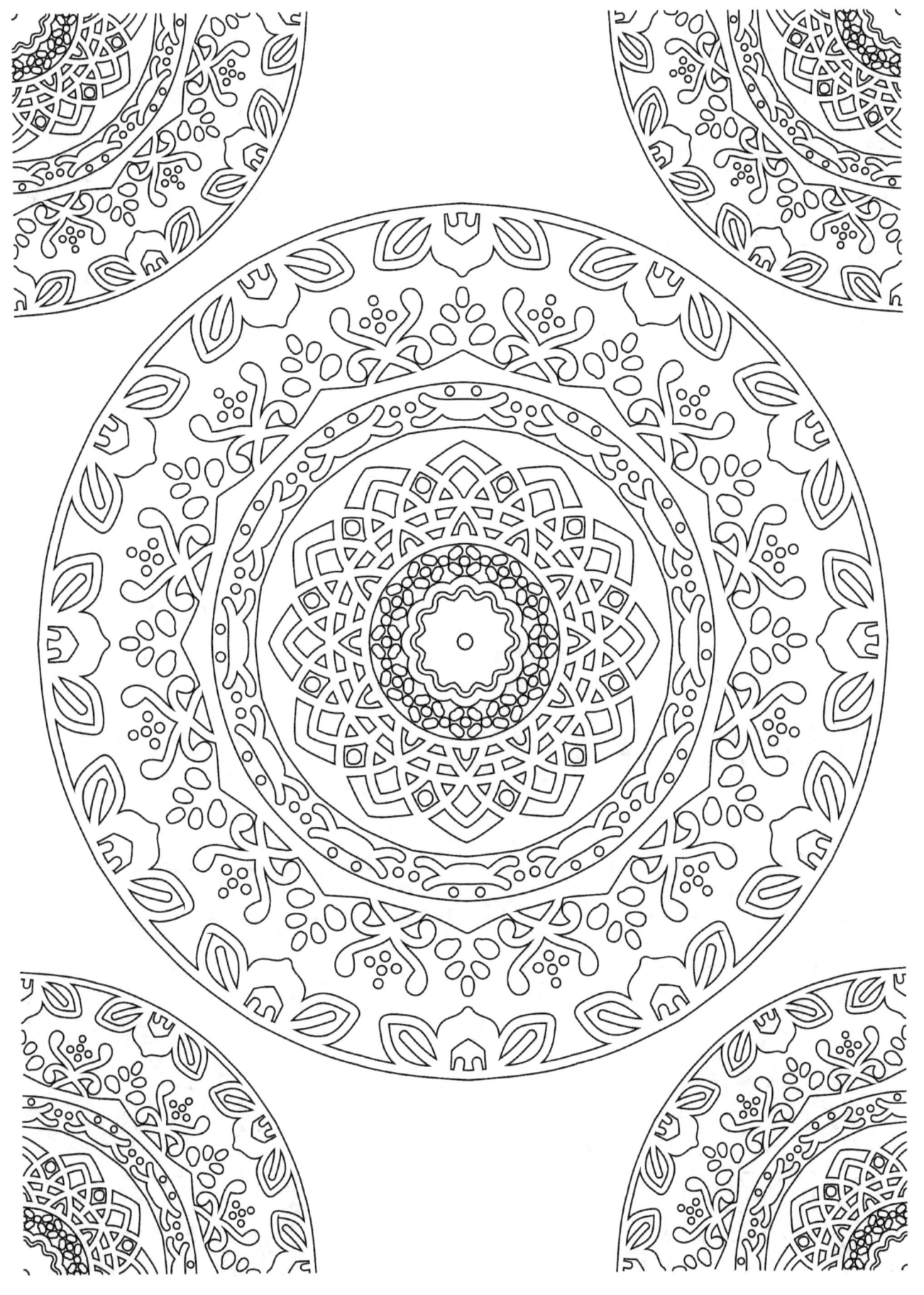

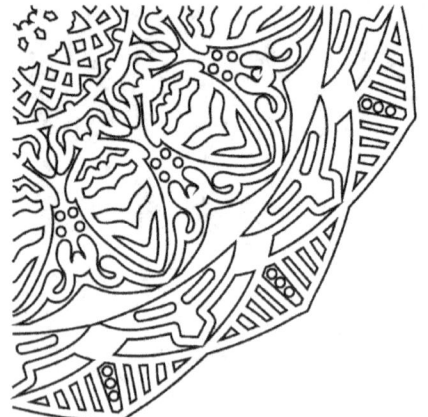
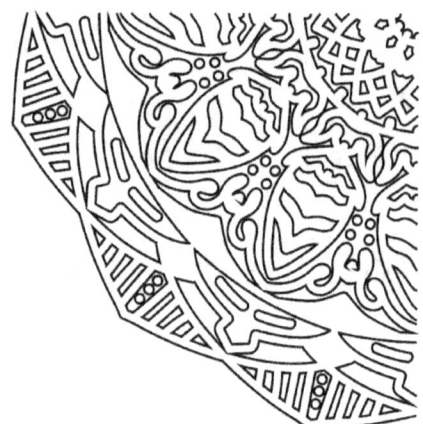

Mandala #38

Coloring a mandala, is a great way to tune into our subconscious and see what emotional and mental state we are in.
These 3 steps will allow you to create a personal mandala:

1. Find a comfortable place to work. Sit in a quiet place where you won't be interrupted. Concentrate on the problem you want to solve the most in the moment.

2. Fill the shape with colors that reflect your current state of mind. Let your imagination run wild. There are no rules when creating a mandala.

3. Take some time to reflect on your mandala and what it means to you, and write down the result below.

_____
_____
_____
_____

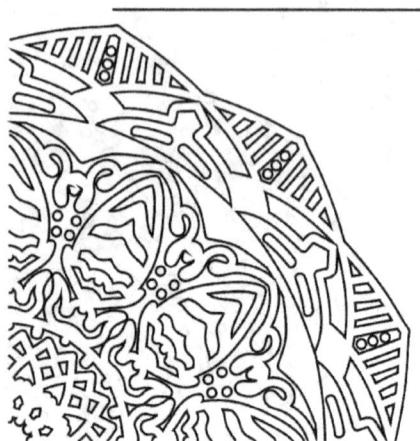
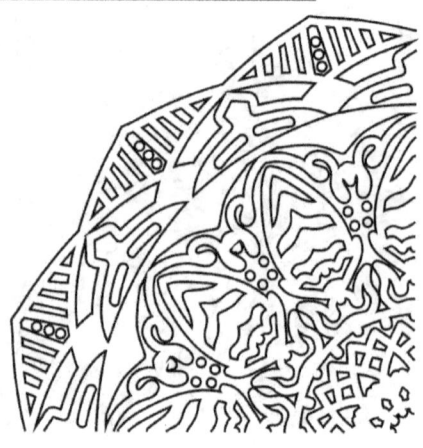

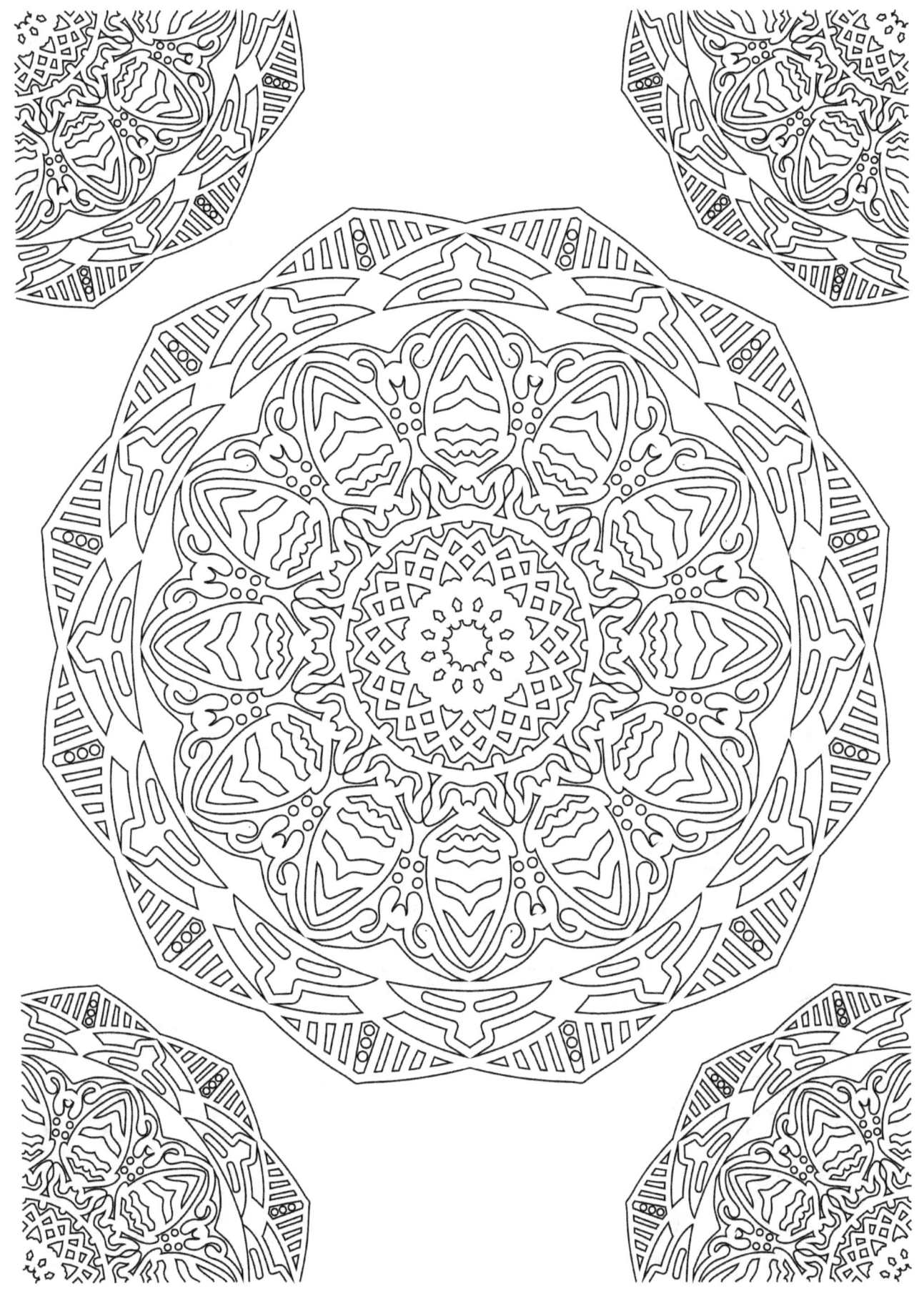

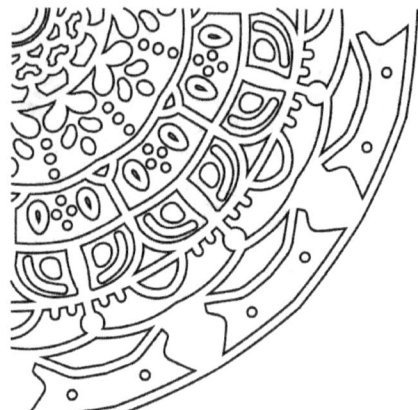
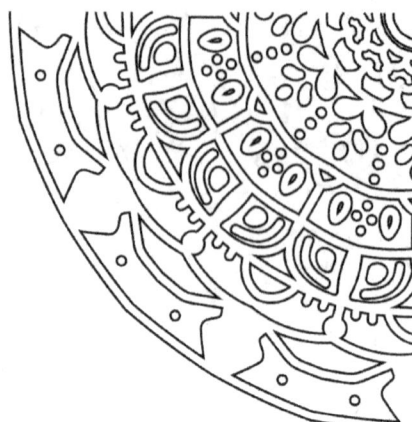

MANDALA #39

Coloring a mandala, is a great way to tune into our subconscious and see what emotional and mental state we are in.

These 3 steps will allow you to create a personal mandala:

1. Find a comfortable place to work. Sit in a quiet place where you won't be interrupted. Concentrate on the problem you want to solve the most in the moment.

2. Fill the shape with colors that reflect your current state of mind. Let your imagination run wild. There are no rules when creating a mandala.

3. Take some time to reflect on your mandala and what it means to you, and write down the result below.

_____

_____

_____

_____

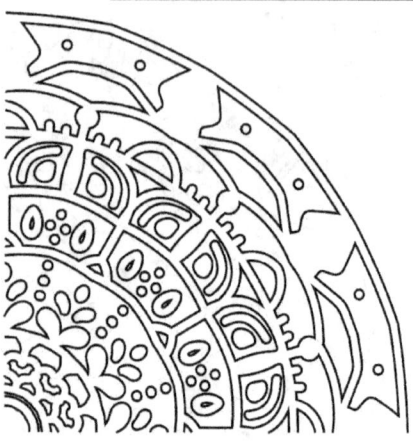
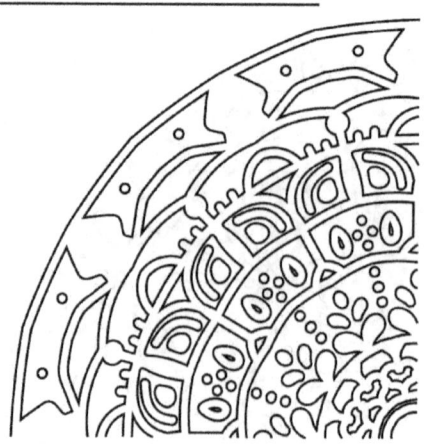

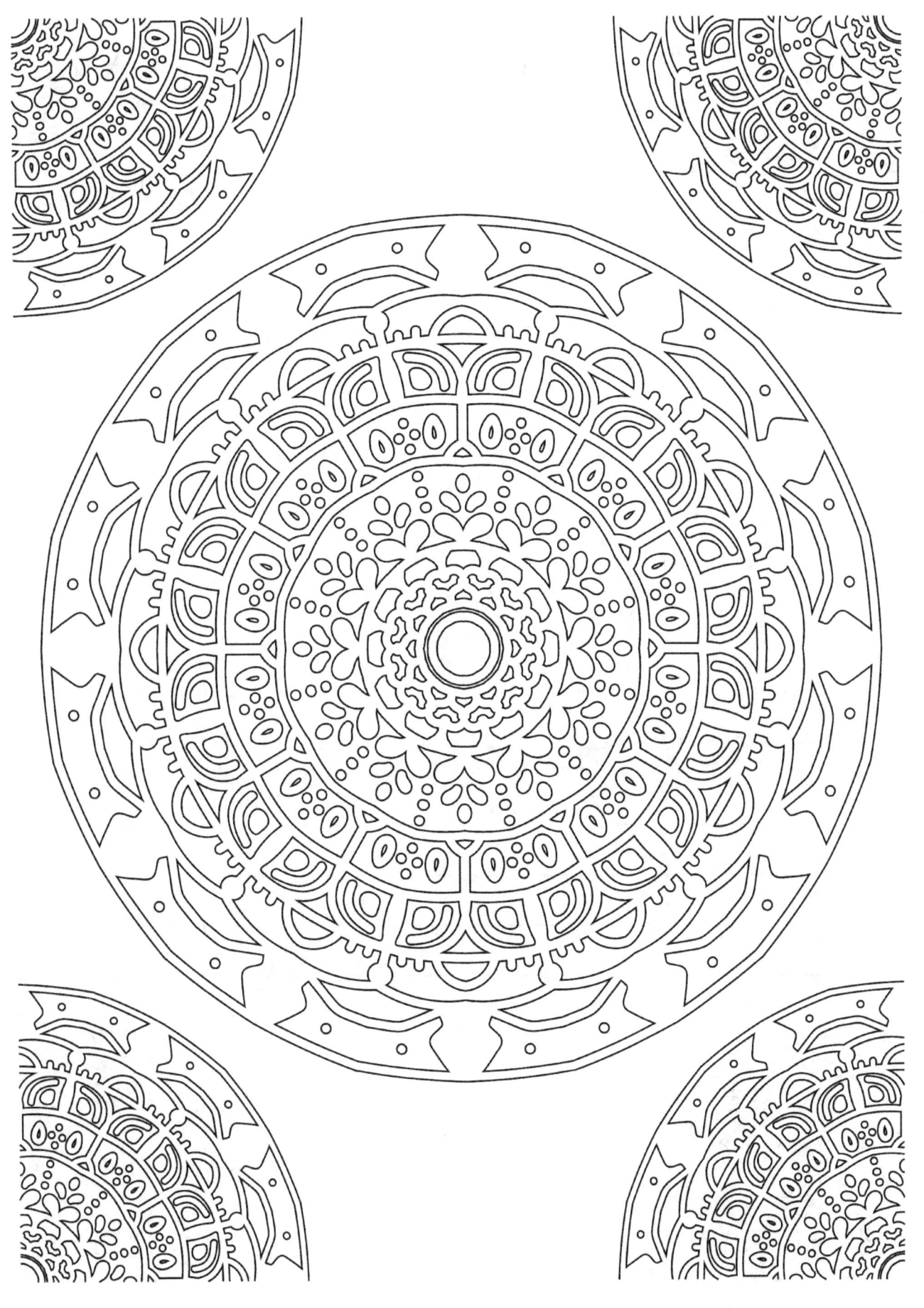

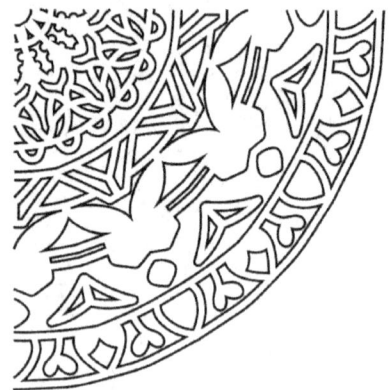
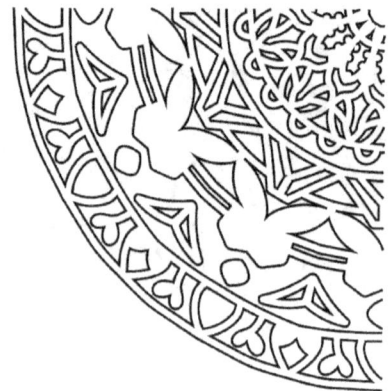

MANDALA #40

Coloring a mandala, is a great way to tune into our subconscious and see what emotional and mental state we are in.
These 3 steps will allow you to create a personal mandala:

1. Find a comfortable place to work. Sit in a quiet place where you won't be interrupted. Concentrate on the problem you want to solve the most in the moment.

2. Fill the shape with colors that reflect your current state of mind. Let your imagination run wild. There are no rules when creating a mandala.

3. Take some time to reflect on your mandala and what it means to you, and write down the result below.

_____
_____
_____
_____

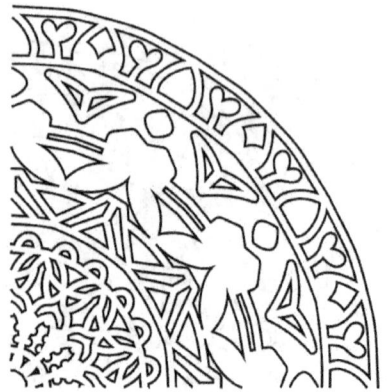
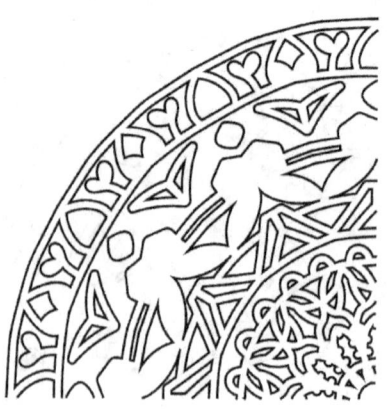

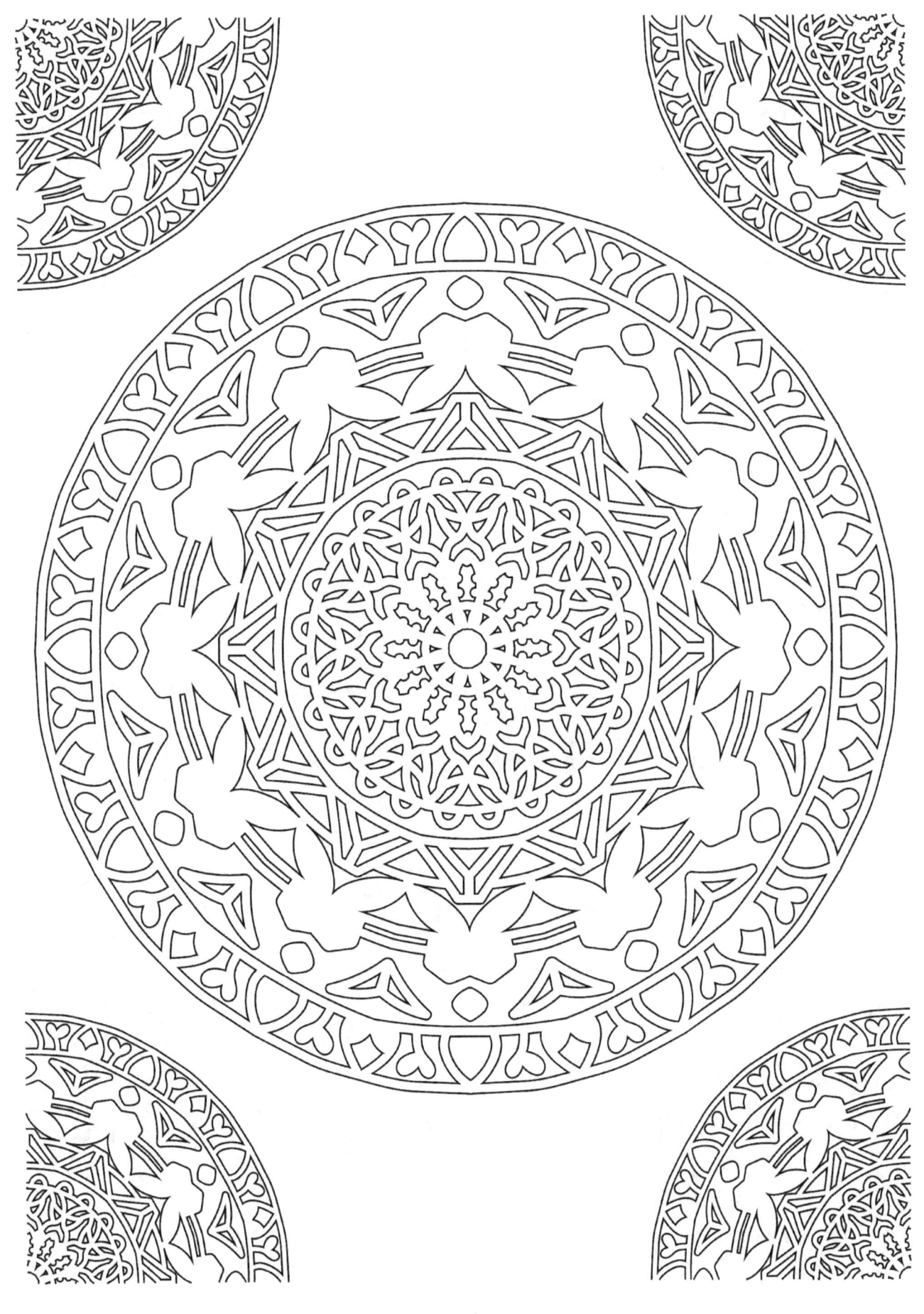

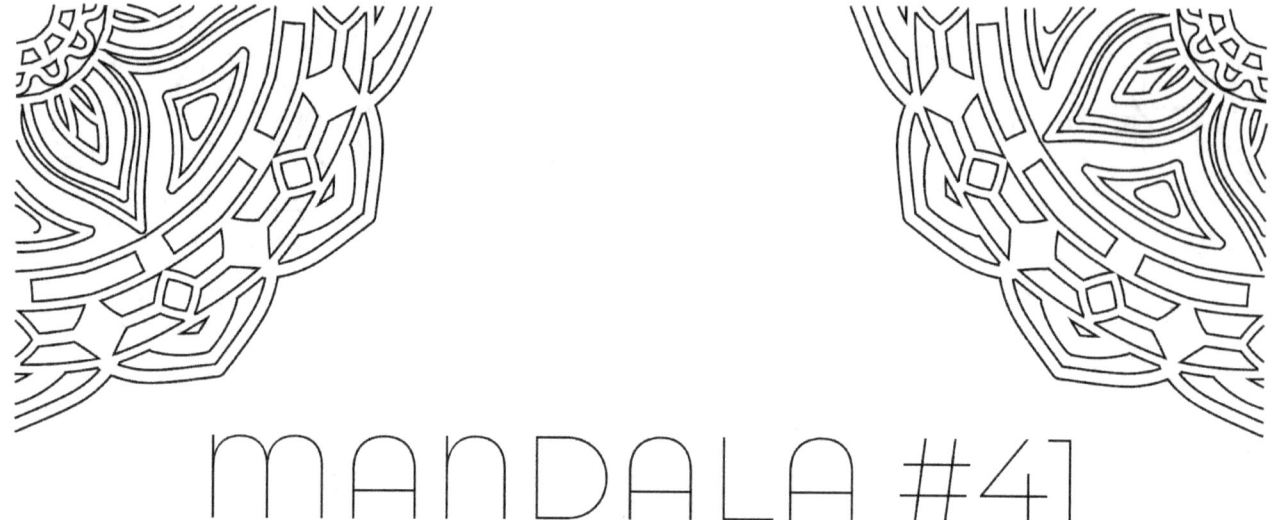

MANDALA #41

Coloring a mandala, is a great way to tune into our subconscious and see what emotional and mental state we are in.

These 3 steps will allow you to create a personal mandala:

1. Find a comfortable place to work. Sit in a quiet place where you won't be interrupted. Concentrate on the problem you want to solve the most in the moment.

2. Fill the shape with colors that reflect your current state of mind. Let your imagination run wild. There are no rules when creating a mandala.

3. Take some time to reflect on your mandala and what it means to you, and write down the result below.

_____

_____

_____

_____

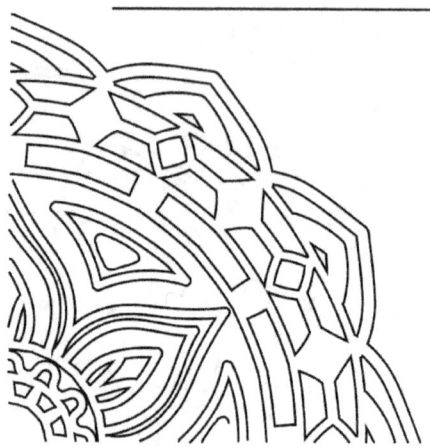
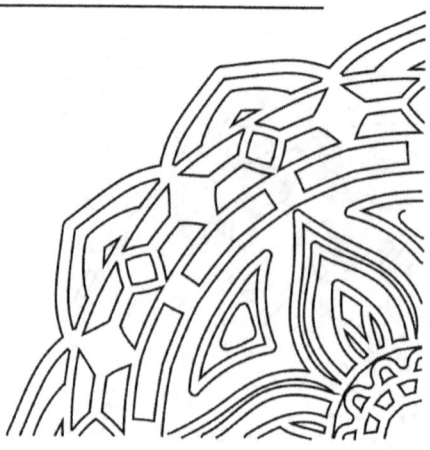

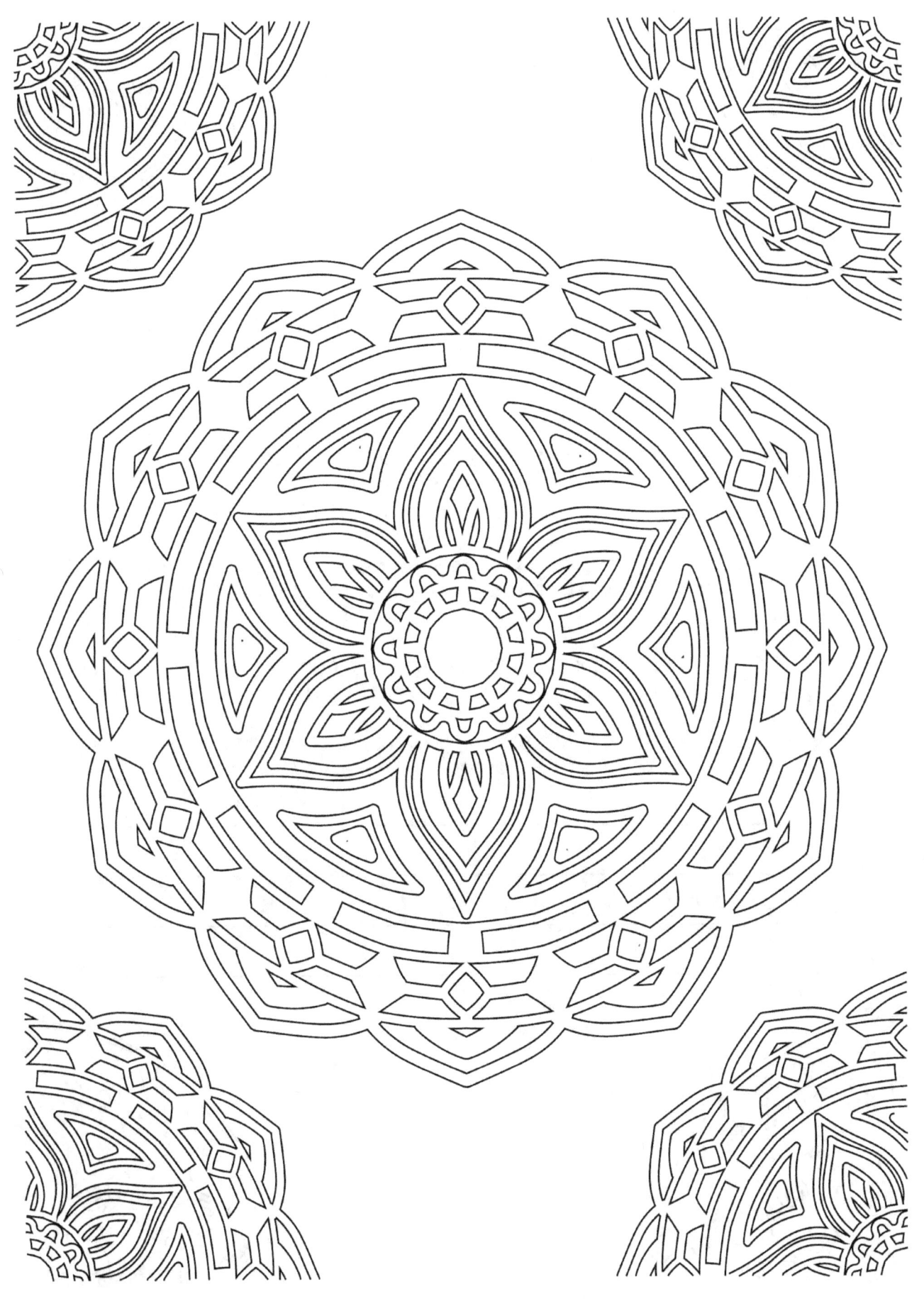

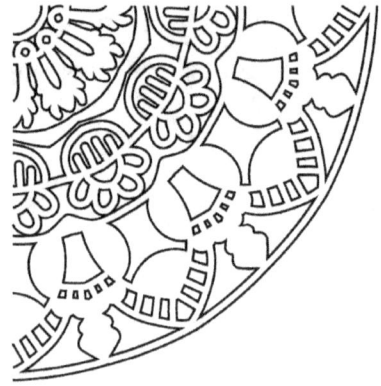 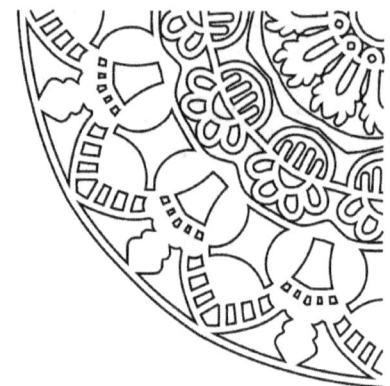

Mandala #42

Coloring a mandala, is a great way to tune into our subconscious and see what emotional and mental state we are in.
These 3 steps will allow you to create a personal mandala:

1. Find a comfortable place to work. Sit in a quiet place where you won't be interrupted. Concentrate on the problem you want to solve the most in the moment.

2. Fill the shape with colors that reflect your current state of mind. Let your imagination run wild. There are no rules when creating a mandala.

3. Take some time to reflect on your mandala and what it means to you, and write down the result below.

_____
_____
_____
_____

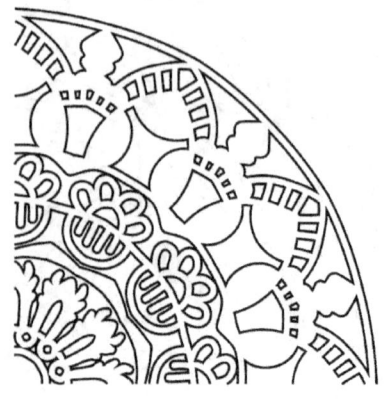 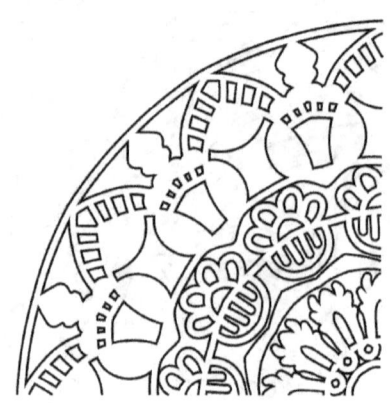

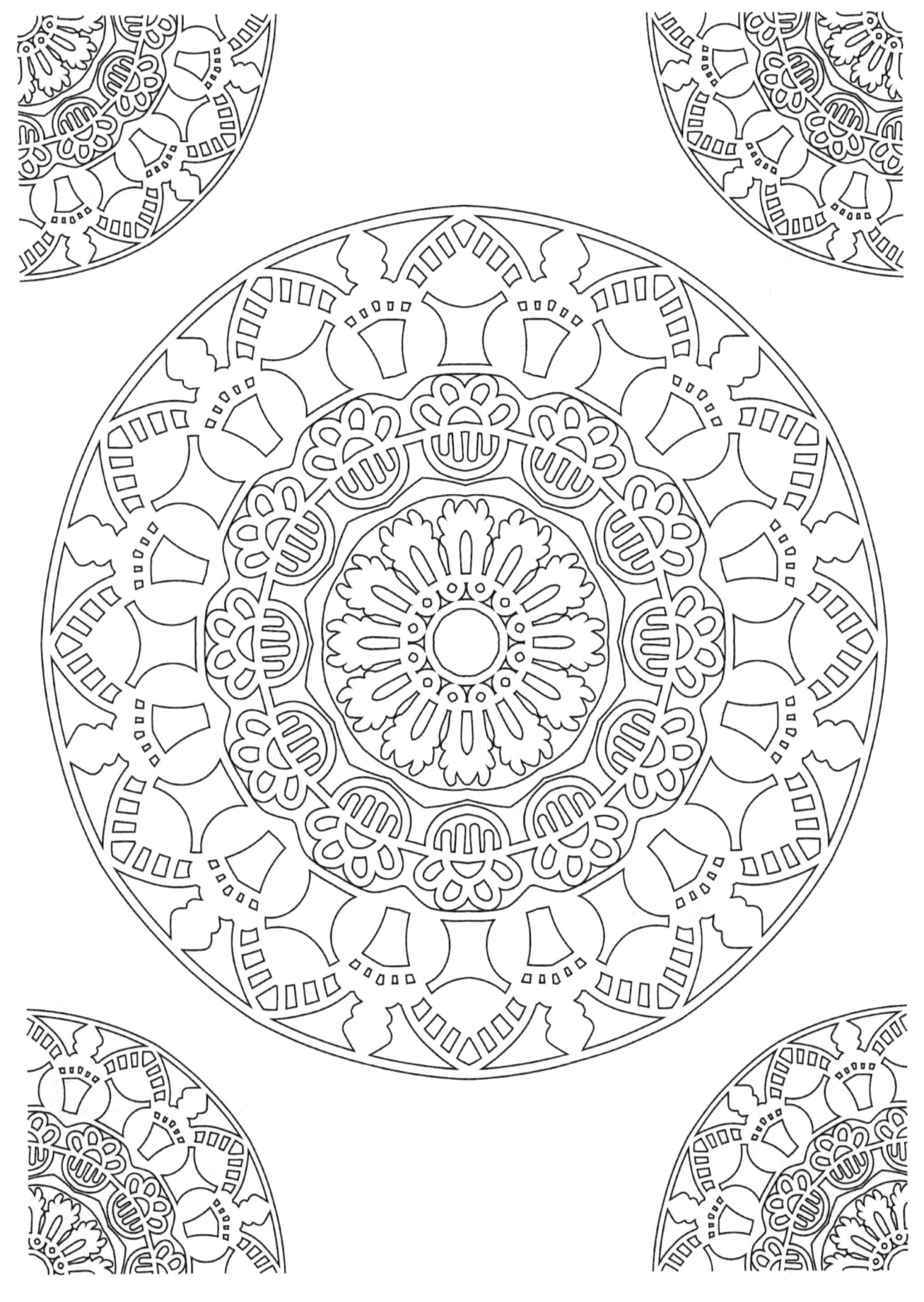

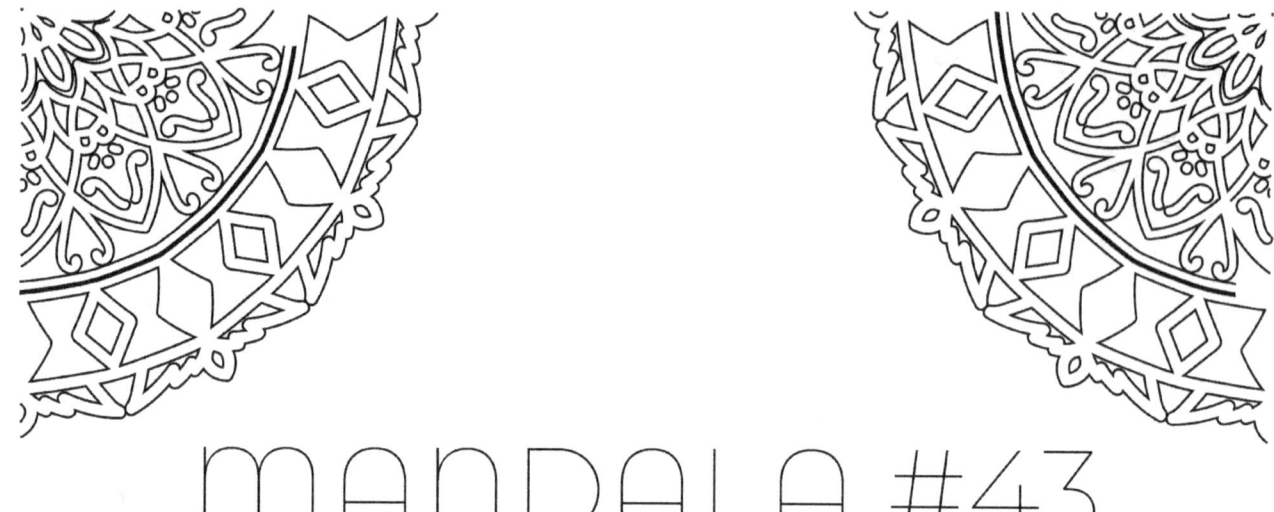

MANDALA #43

Coloring a mandala, is a great way to tune into our subconscious and see what emotional and mental state we are in.

These 3 steps will allow you to create a personal mandala:

1. Find a comfortable place to work. Sit in a quiet place where you won't be interrupted. Concentrate on the problem you want to solve the most in the moment.

2. Fill the shape with colors that reflect your current state of mind. Let your imagination run wild. There are no rules when creating a mandala.

3. Take some time to reflect on your mandala and what it means to you, and write down the result below.

_____

_____

_____

_____

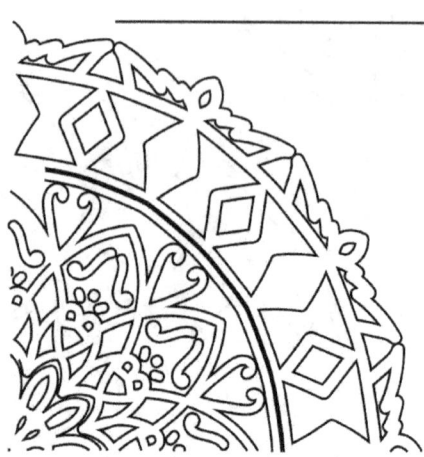
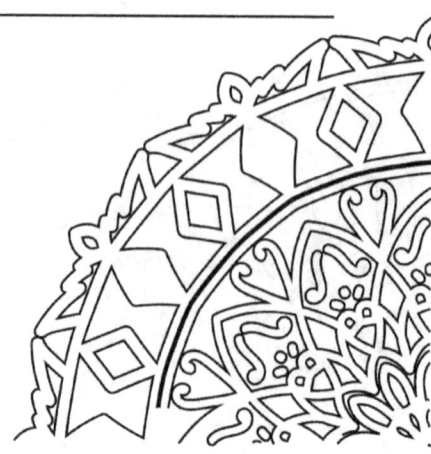

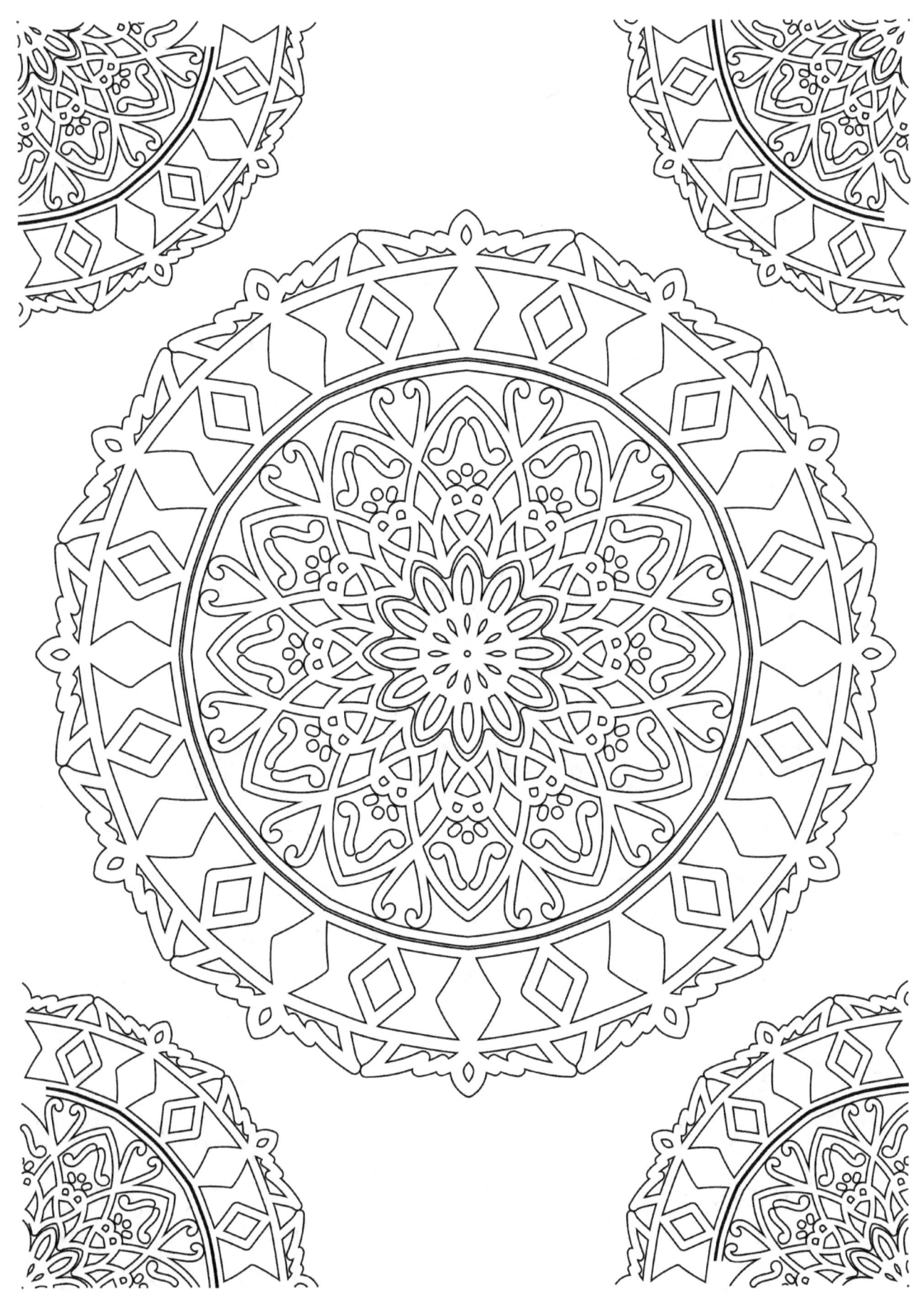

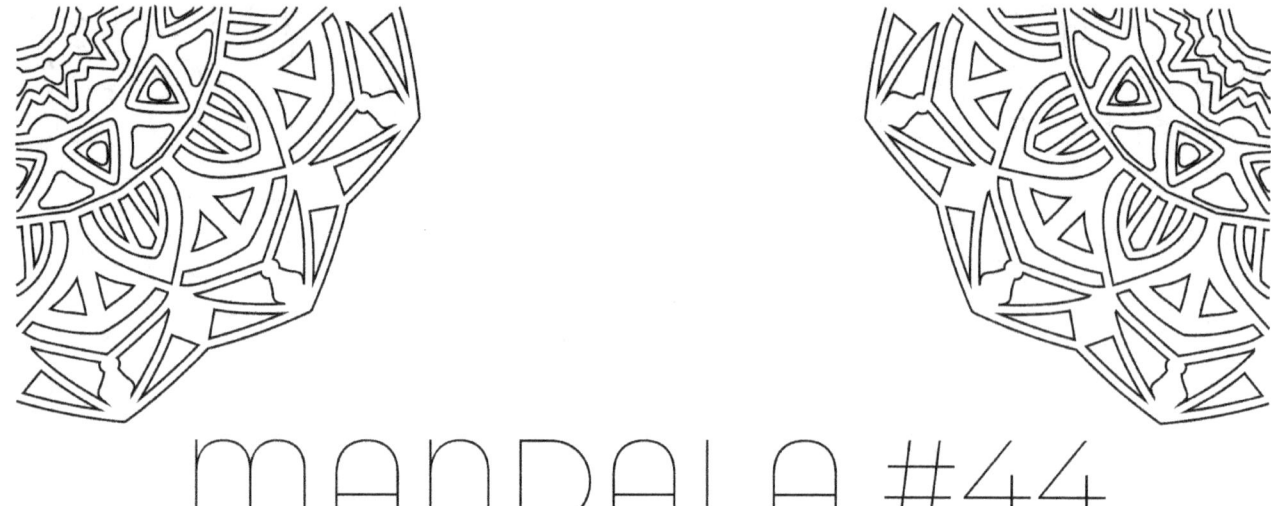

MANDALA #44

Coloring a mandala, is a great way to tune into our subconscious and see what emotional and mental state we are in.
These 3 steps will allow you to create a personal mandala:

1. Find a comfortable place to work. Sit in a quiet place where you won't be interrupted. Concentrate on the problem you want to solve the most in the moment.

2. Fill the shape with colors that reflect your current state of mind. Let your imagination run wild. There are no rules when creating a mandala.

3. Take some time to reflect on your mandala and what it means to you, and write down the result below.

_____
_____
_____
_____

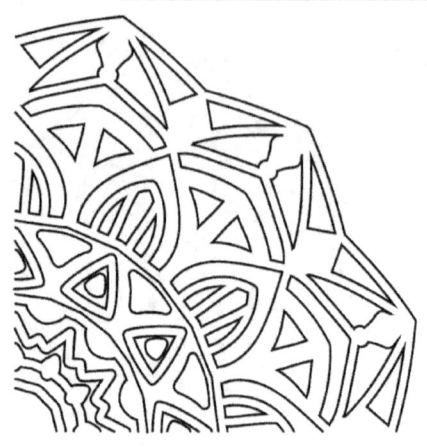
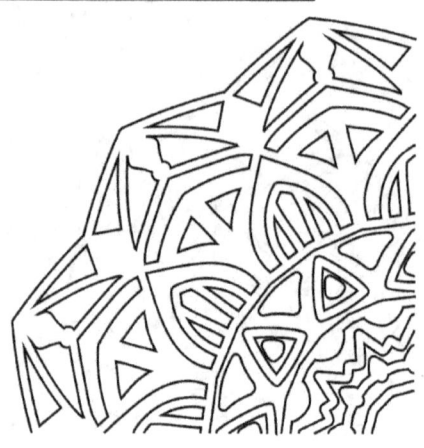

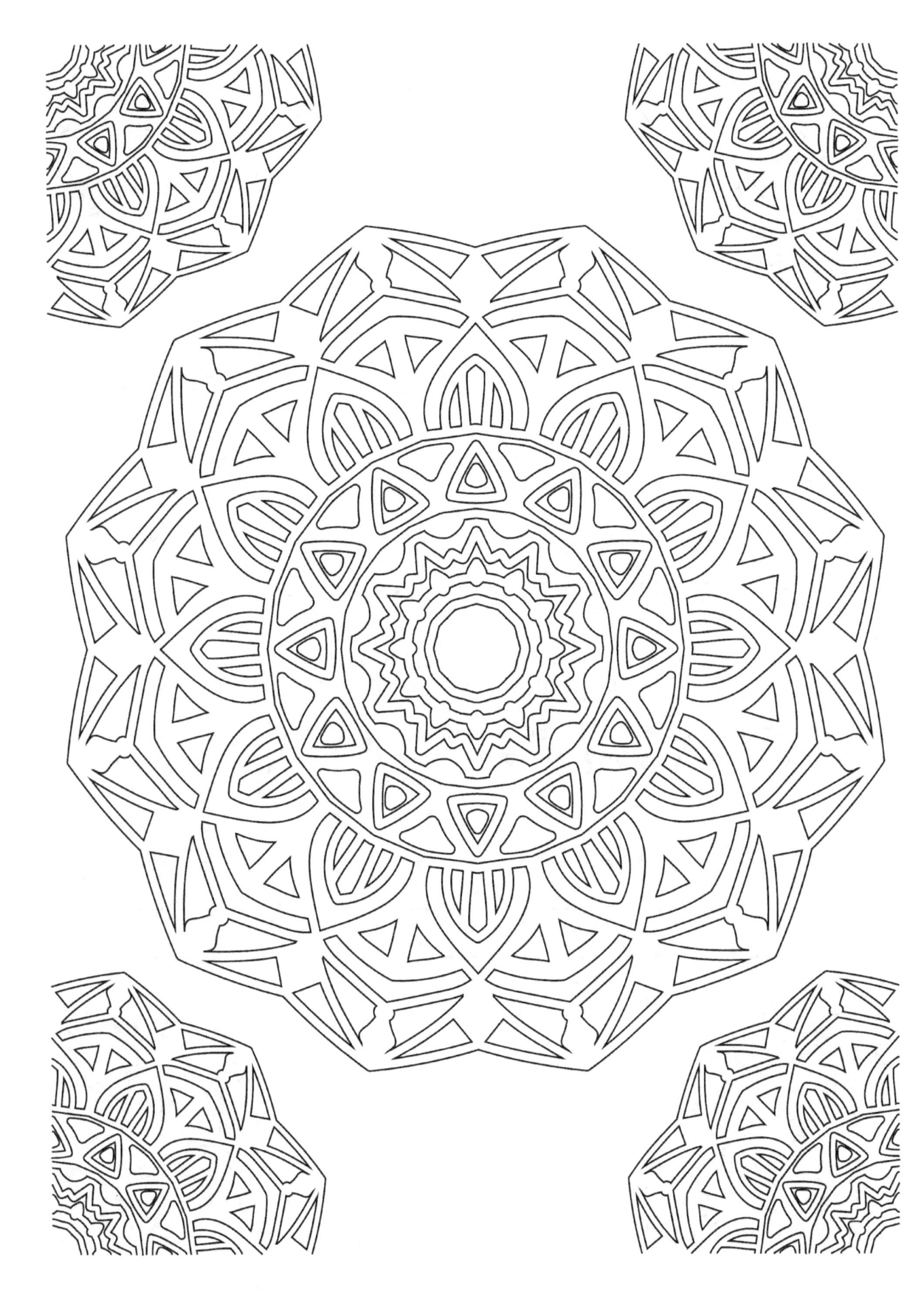

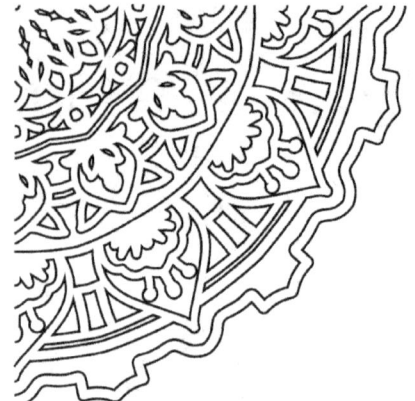
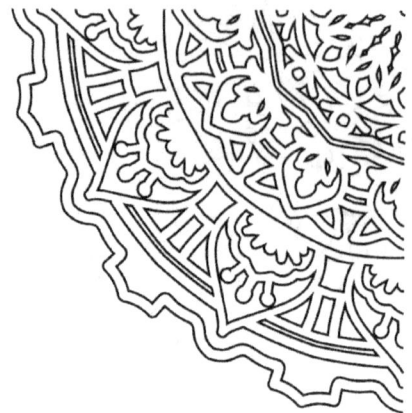

MANDALA #45

Coloring a mandala, is a great way to tune into our subconscious and see what emotional and mental state we are in.

These 3 steps will allow you to create a personal mandala:

1. Find a comfortable place to work. Sit in a quiet place where you won't be interrupted. Concentrate on the problem you want to solve the most in the moment.

2. Fill the shape with colors that reflect your current state of mind. Let your imagination run wild. There are no rules when creating a mandala.

3. Take some time to reflect on your mandala and what it means to you, and write down the result below.

_____

_____

_____

_____

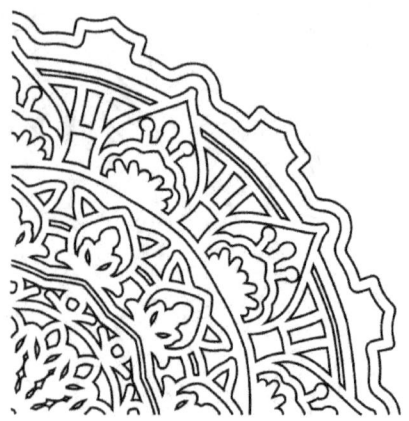
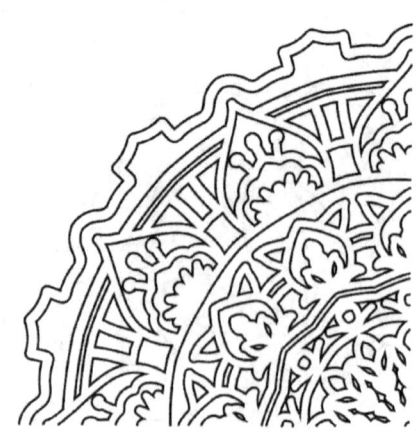

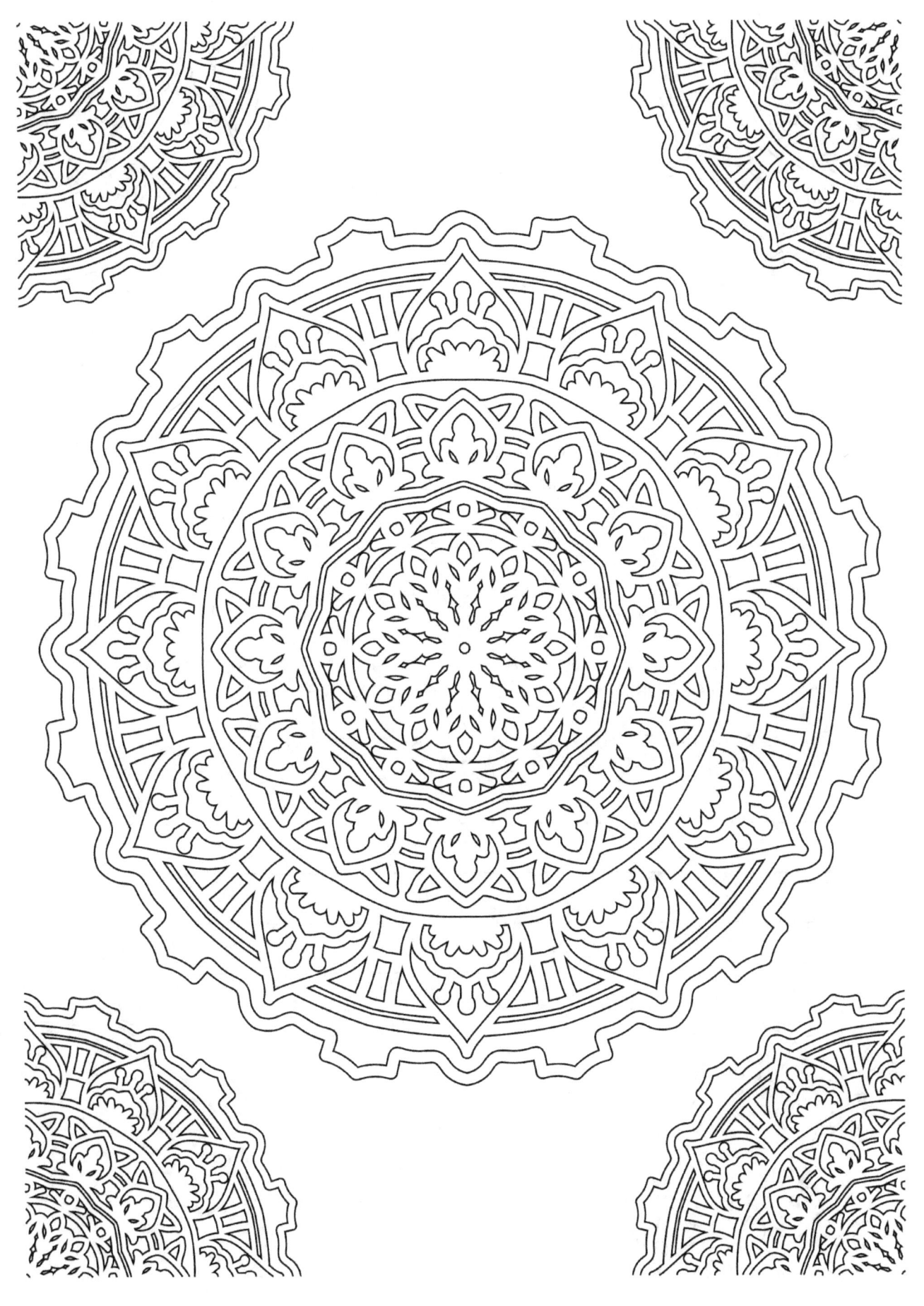

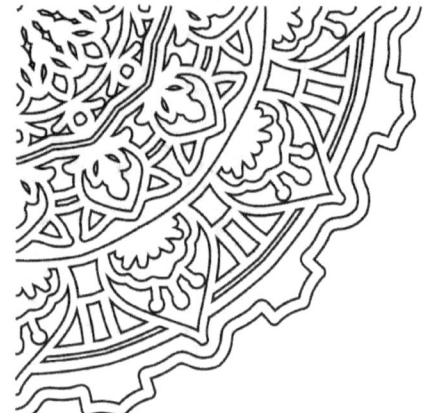
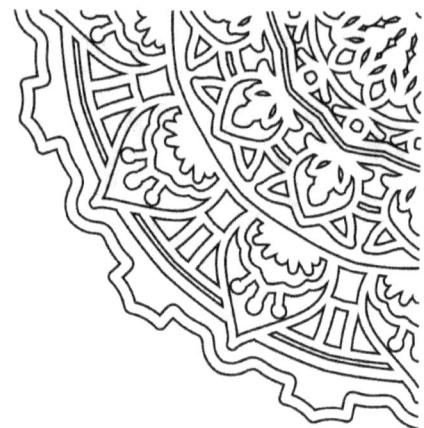

MANDALA #46

Coloring a mandala, is a great way to tune into our subconscious and see what emotional and mental state we are in.
These 3 steps will allow you to create a personal mandala:

1. Find a comfortable place to work. Sit in a quiet place where you won't be interrupted. Concentrate on the problem you want to solve the most in the moment.

2. Fill the shape with colors that reflect your current state of mind. Let your imagination run wild. There are no rules when creating a mandala.

3. Take some time to reflect on your mandala and what it means to you, and write down the result below.

_____
_____
_____
_____

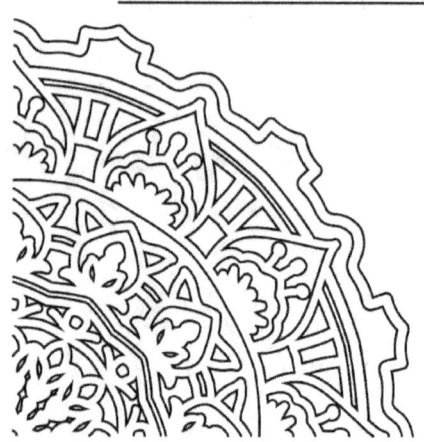
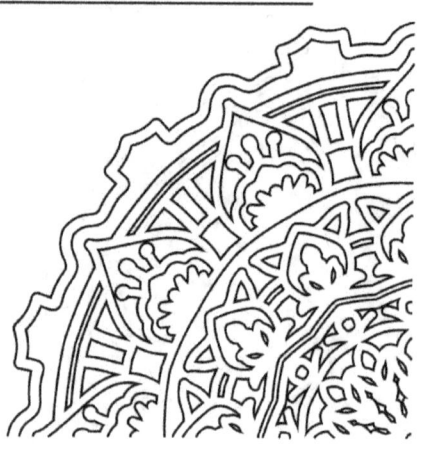

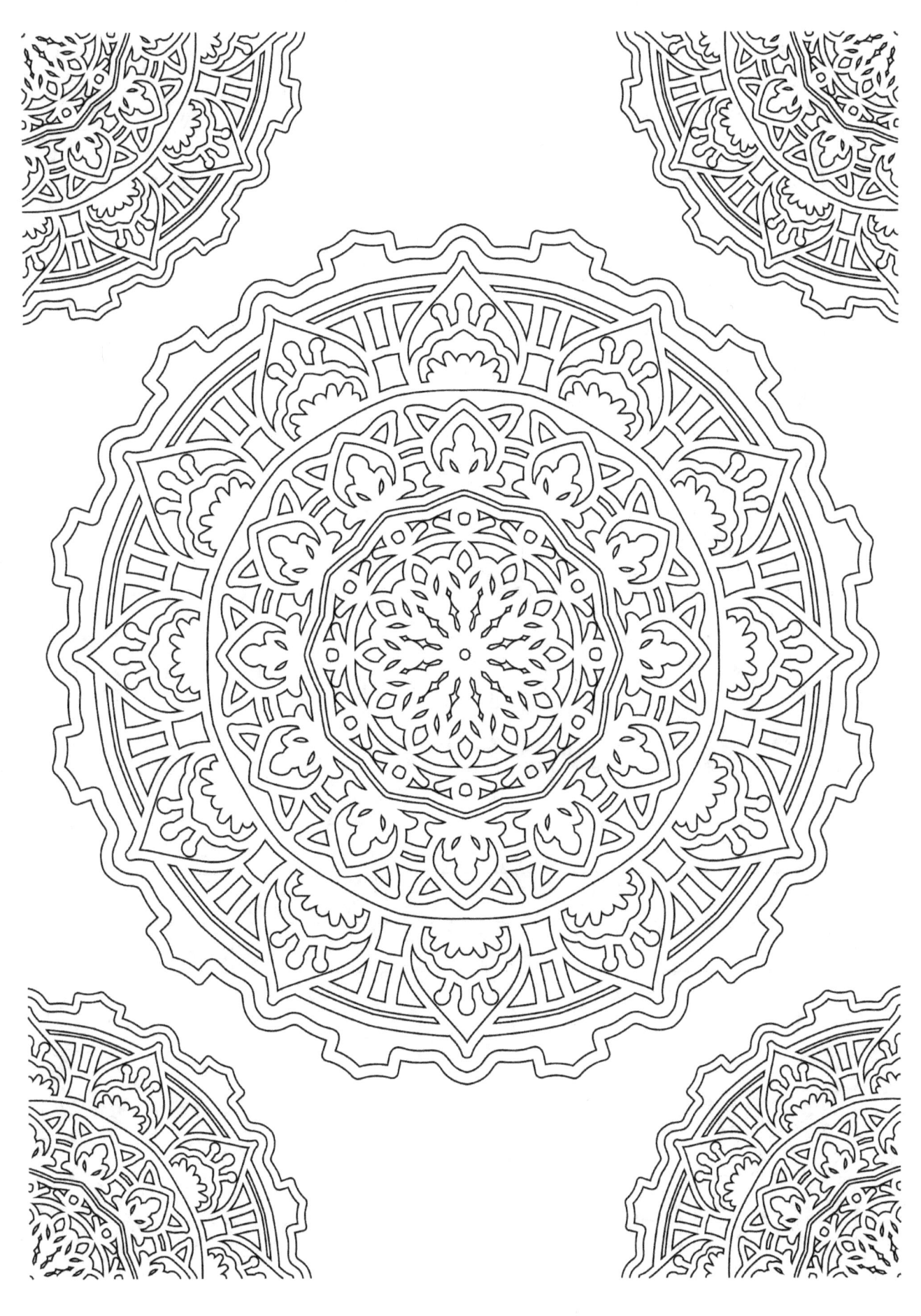

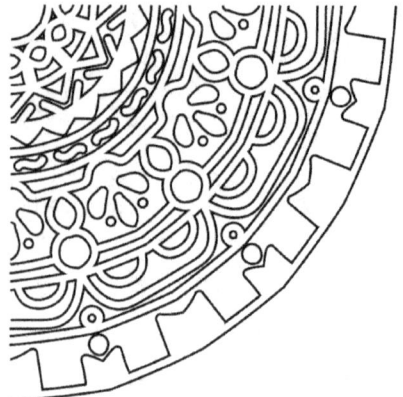
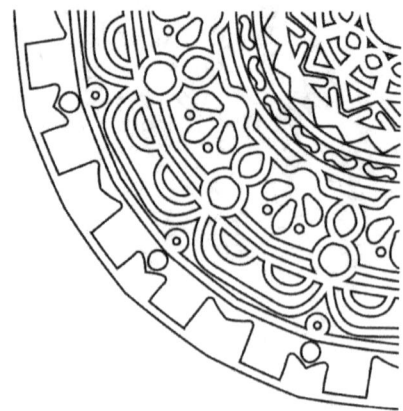

MANDALA #47

Coloring a mandala, is a great way to tune into our subconscious and see what emotional and mental state we are in.

These 3 steps will allow you to create a personal mandala:

1. Find a comfortable place to work. Sit in a quiet place where you won't be interrupted. Concentrate on the problem you want to solve the most in the moment.

2. Fill the shape with colors that reflect your current state of mind. Let your imagination run wild. There are no rules when creating a mandala.

3. Take some time to reflect on your mandala and what it means to you, and write down the result below.

_____

_____

_____

_____

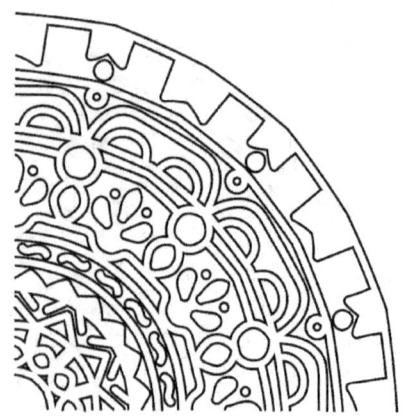
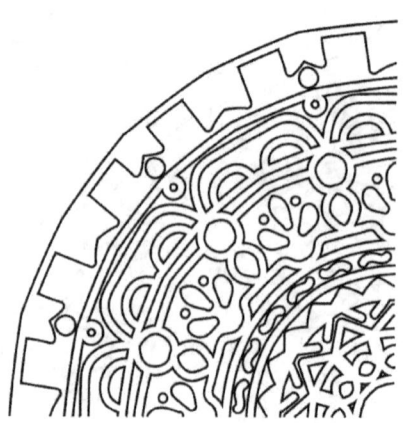

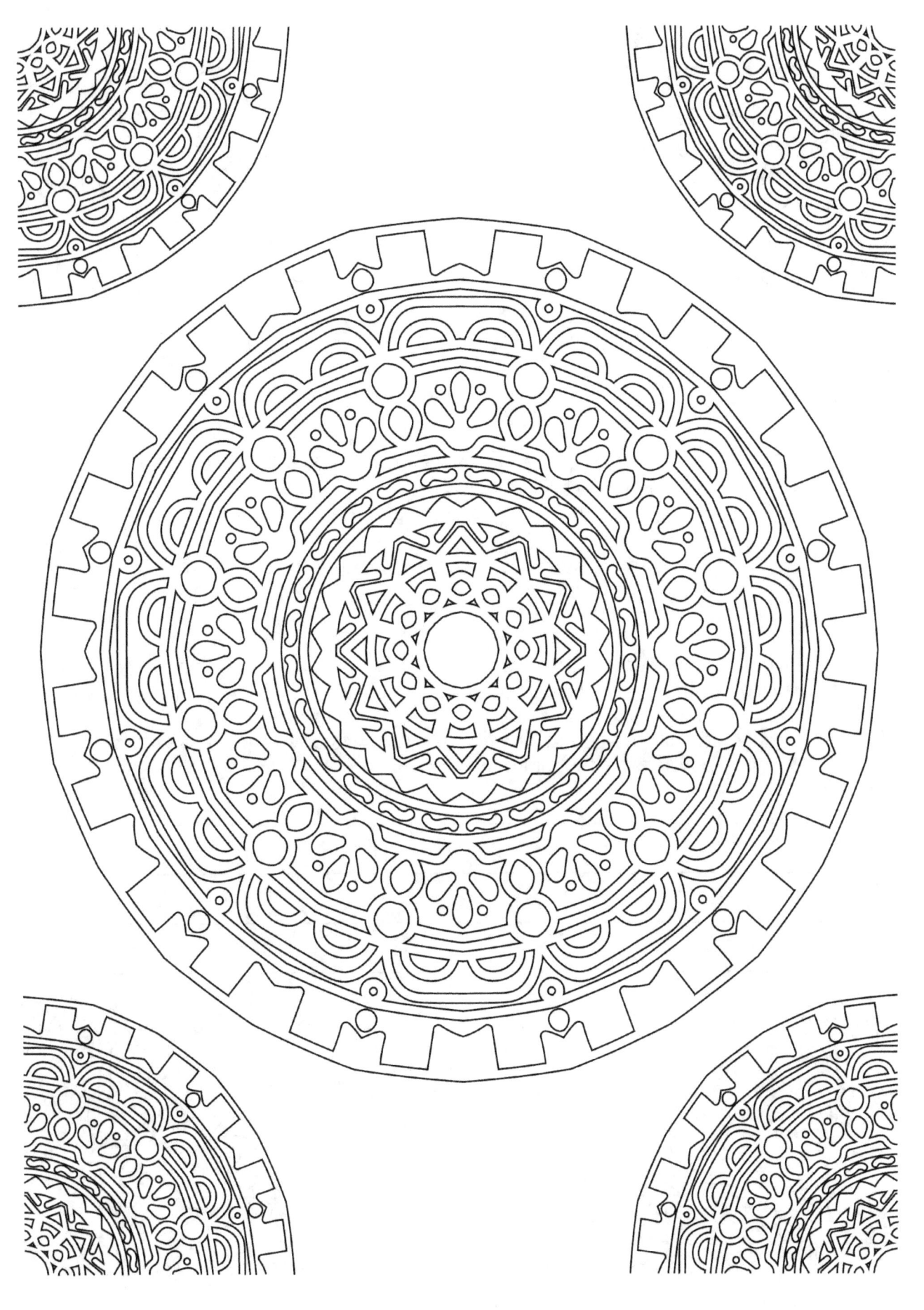

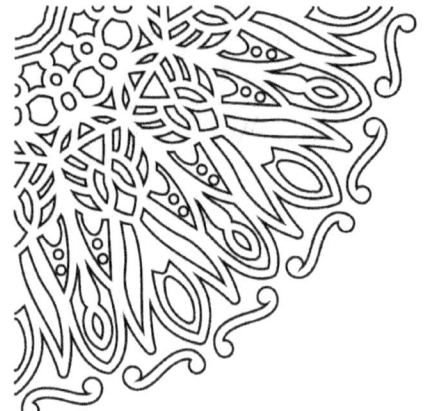
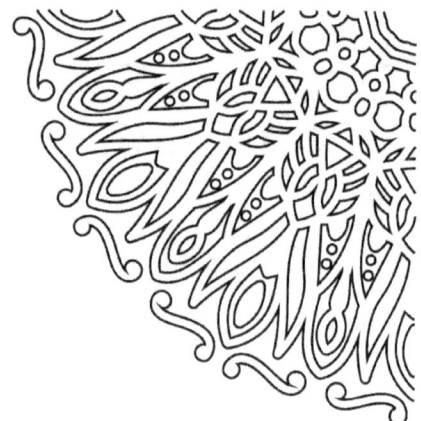

MANDALA #48

Coloring a mandala, is a great way to tune into our subconscious and see what emotional and mental state we are in.
These 3 steps will allow you to create a personal mandala:

1. Find a comfortable place to work. Sit in a quiet place where you won't be interrupted. Concentrate on the problem you want to solve the most in the moment.

2. Fill the shape with colors that reflect your current state of mind. Let your imagination run wild. There are no rules when creating a mandala.

3. Take some time to reflect on your mandala and what it means to you, and write down the result below.

_____
_____
_____
_____

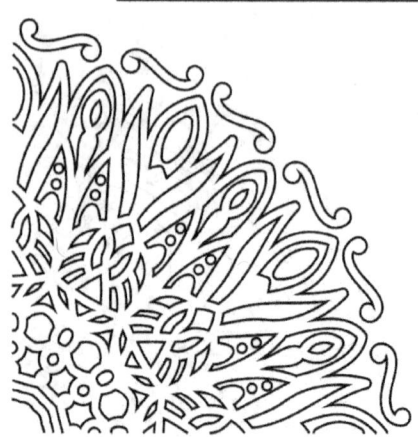
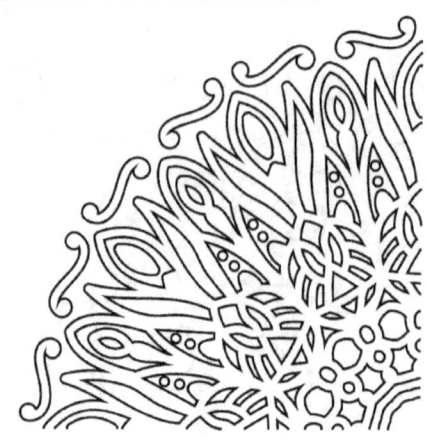

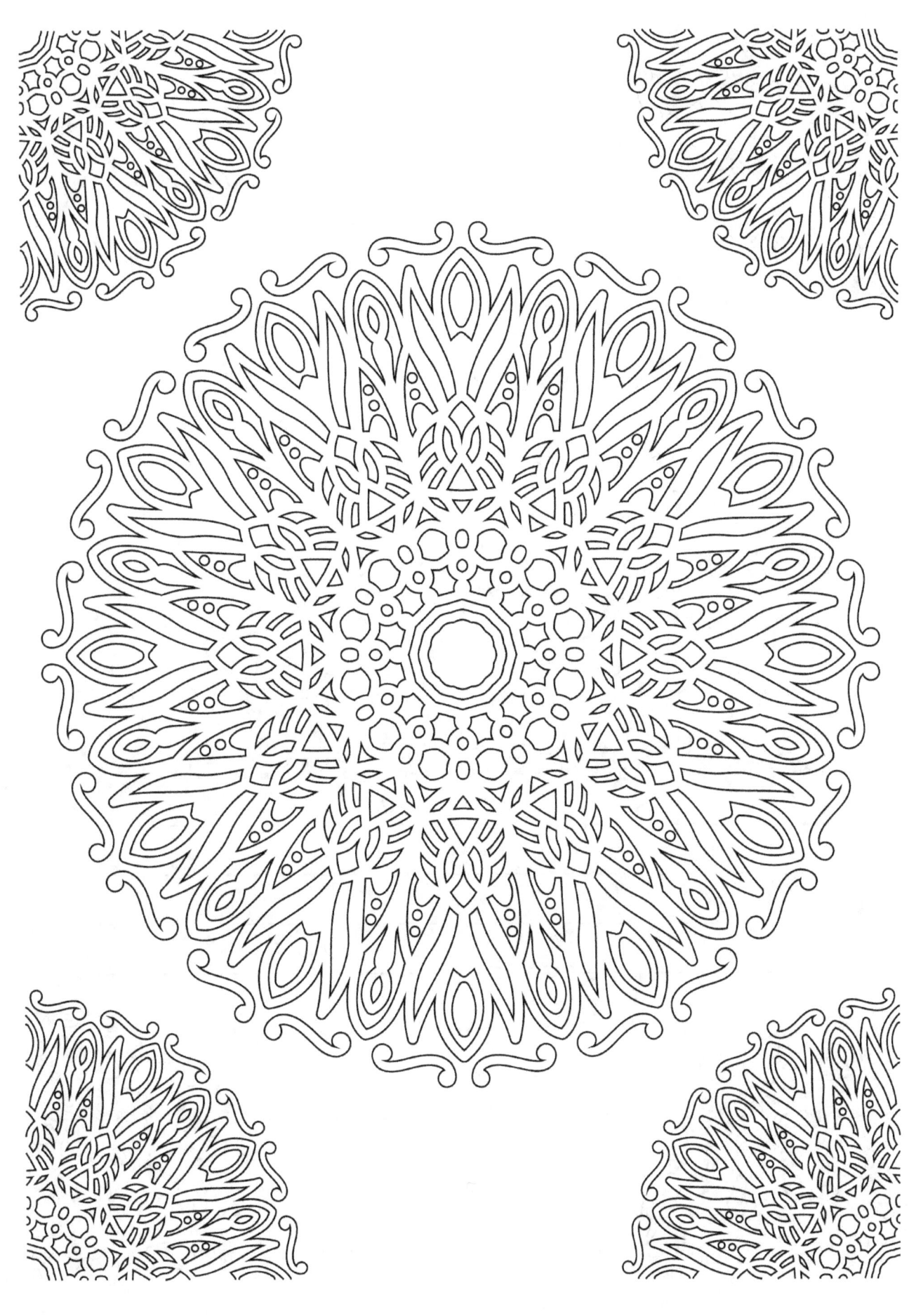

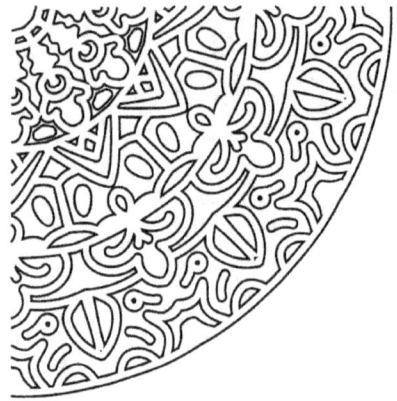
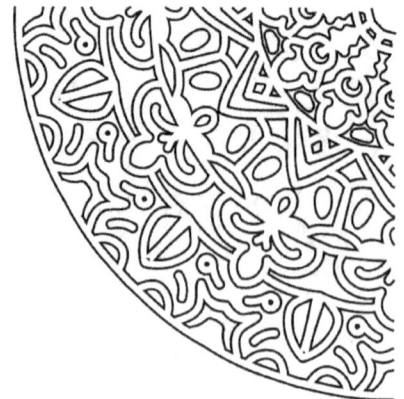

MANDALA #49

Coloring a mandala, is a great way to tune into our subconscious and see what emotional and mental state we are in.
These 3 steps will allow you to create a personal mandala:

1. Find a comfortable place to work. Sit in a quiet place where you won't be interrupted. Concentrate on the problem you want to solve the most in the moment.

2. Fill the shape with colors that reflect your current state of mind. Let your imagination run wild. There are no rules when creating a mandala.

3. Take some time to reflect on your mandala and what it means to you, and write down the result below.

_____

_____

_____

_____

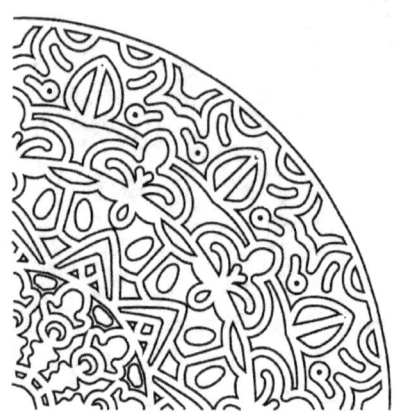
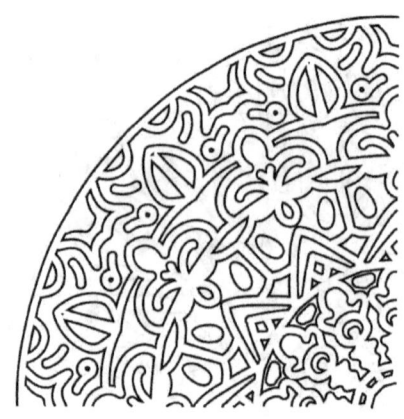

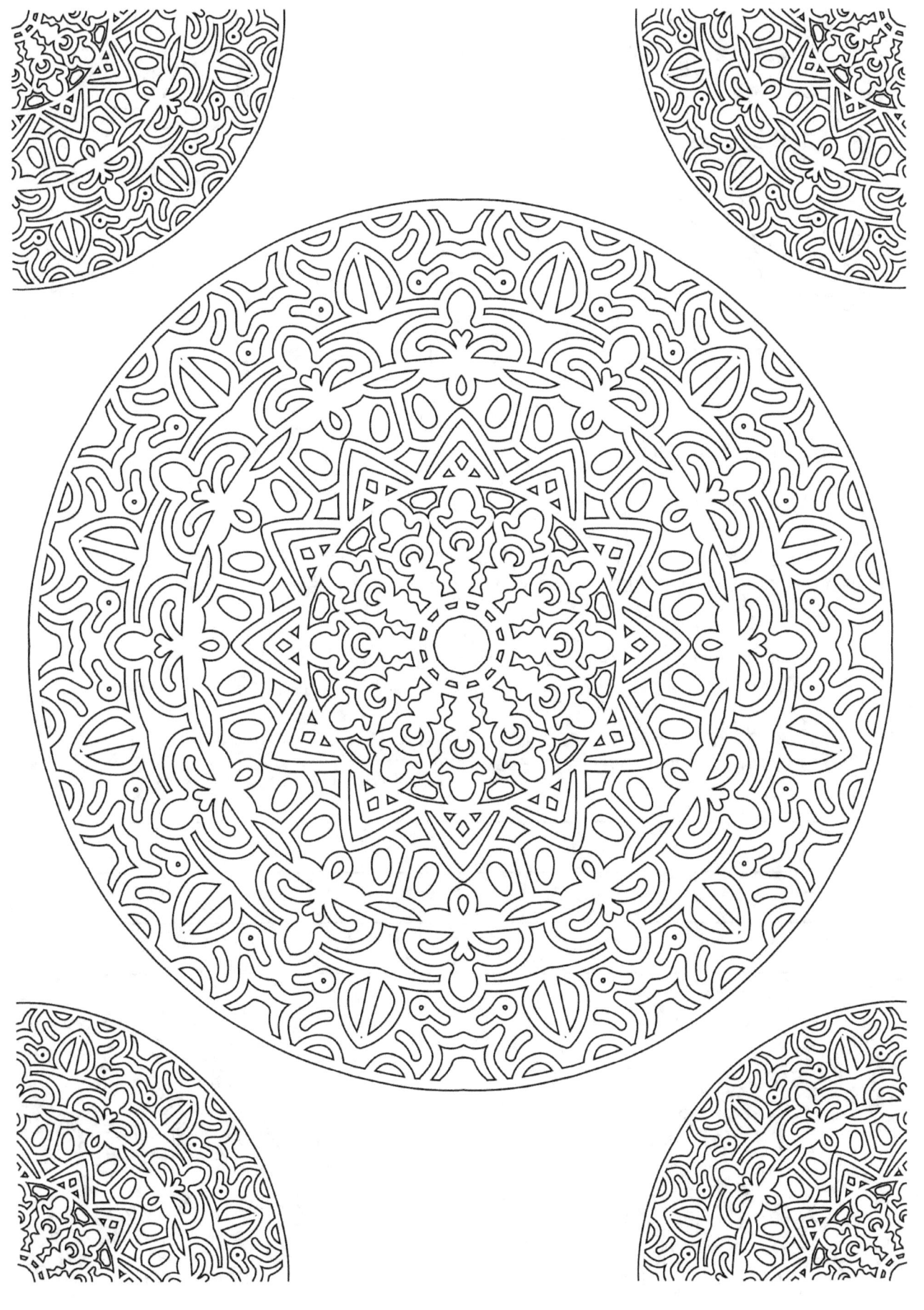

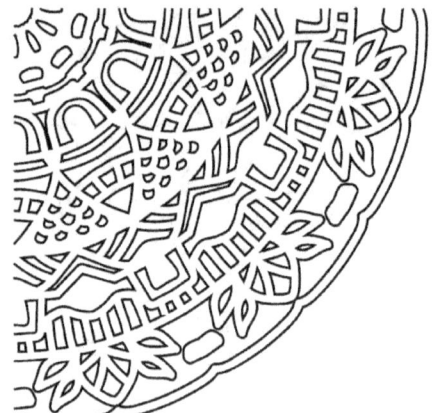
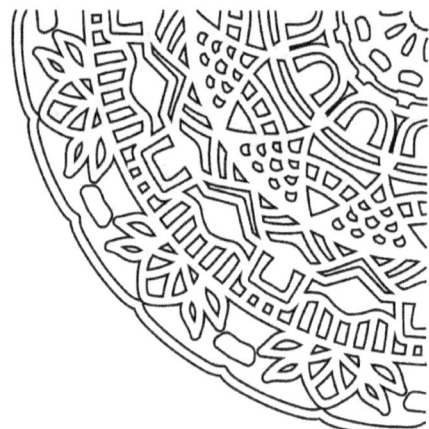

MANDALA #50

Coloring a mandala, is a great way to tune into our subconscious and see what emotional and mental state we are in.

These 3 steps will allow you to create a personal mandala:

1. Find a comfortable place to work. Sit in a quiet place where you won't be interrupted. Concentrate on the problem you want to solve the most in the moment.

2. Fill the shape with colors that reflect your current state of mind. Let your imagination run wild. There are no rules when creating a mandala.

3. Take some time to reflect on your mandala and what it means to you, and write down the result below.

_____
_____
_____
_____

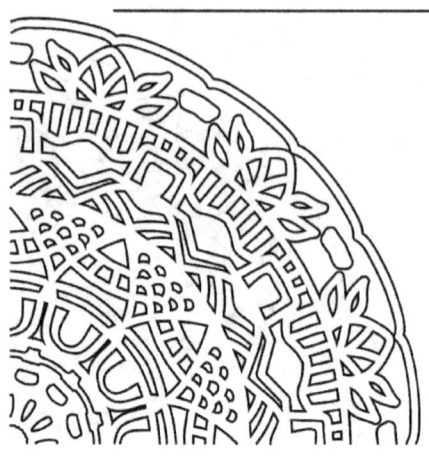
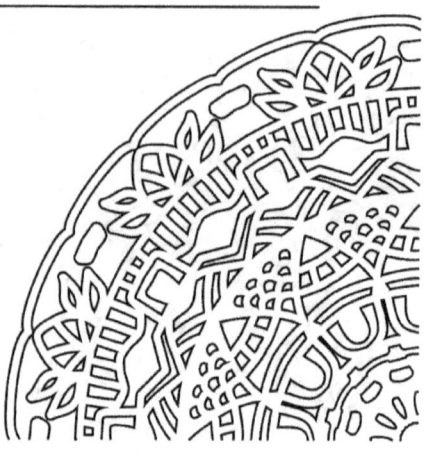

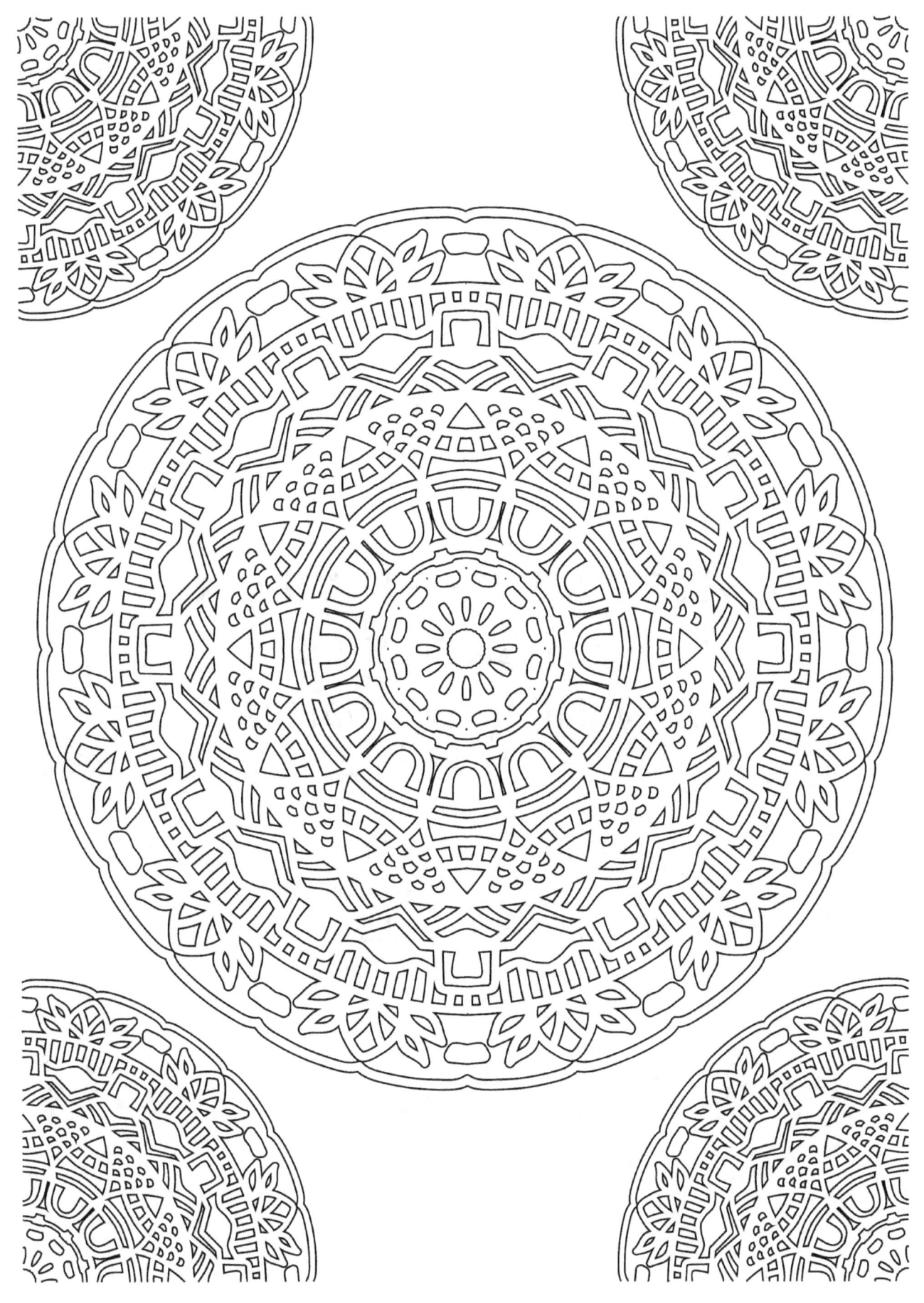

Discover the healing properties of personal mandalas

www.ingramcontent.com/pod-product-compliance
Lightning Source LLC
Chambersburg PA
CBHW081101240526
45465CB00026B/3021